SECRETS OF THE SUN

21st Century Essays
David Lazar and Patrick Madden, Series Editors

SECRETS
OF THE SUN

A Memoir

Mako Yoshikawa

MAD CREEK BOOKS, AN IMPRINT OF
THE OHIO STATE UNIVERSITY PRESS
COLUMBUS

Published by Mad Creek Books, an imprint of The Ohio State University Press.

Library of Congress Cataloging-in-Publication Data

Names: Yoshikawa, Mako, author.

Title: Secrets of the sun : a memoir / Mako Yoshikawa.

Other titles: 21st century essays.

Description: Columbus : Mad Creek Books, an imprint of The Ohio State University Press, [2024] | Series: 21st century essays | Summary: "A memoir about a daughter trying to understand her father's genius, mental illness, violence, and past. Touches on Japanese culture, immigration, racism, WWII, and the Asian American experience"—Provided by publisher.

Identifiers: LCCN 2023038948 | ISBN 9780814258934 (paperback) | ISBN 081425893X (paperback) | ISBN 9780814283202 (ebook) | ISBN 0814283209 (ebook)

Subjects: LCSH: Yoshikawa, Mako—Family. | Yoshikawa, Shōichi, 1935–2010—Relations with women. | Mentally ill fathers—Biography. | Physicists—Biography. | Fathers and daughters. | Novelists, American—20th century—Family relationships.

Classification: LCC PS3575.O645 Z46 2024 | DDC 813/.54 [B]—dc23/eng/20230921

LC record available at https://lccn.loc.gov/2023038948

Cover design by Charles Brock

Text design by Stuart Rodriguez

Type set in Adobe Caslon

For my mother, Hiroko Sherwin

CONTENTS

DEARLY BELOVED

The rehearsal dinner was in five hours, and people were converging. I saw them as blips on a radar screen, blinking on off on off as they drew close. My mother and stepfather, fresh off a flight from England. The guests that my fiancé, Rob, was picking up at the airport. My sisters and their children and partners, still on planes from California and China. Rob's two kids, being ferried over by his ex, and my three stepsisters and their families, also in cars. Two grad school friends of mine from Europe who were already here, catching up in the kitchen; numerous other friends and relatives. I was eager to be with them, to have the blips that were Rob and me surrounded and then submerged by all those points of light, but I needed more time. On the floor in our walk-in, I was dumping out jewelry boxes in a frantic search for the earrings my best friend had given me to wear at the wedding.

When my cell rang and I had to scramble for it on the high shelf where I'd stashed it, I was so boxed in I almost did a face-plant.

On the phone, a number that began with 609, the area code of Princeton, New Jersey, my old hometown.

When the speaker identified himself as a member of the Princeton police force, my first thought was that I'd gotten yet another ticket—that when Rob and I had driven to Princeton seven months earlier so I could finally introduce him to my father, I'd been clocked once again at ninety plus.

The cop asked me to verify my name and address.

I did so and said, "If this is about a ticket, can I pay it online?"

"What?"

"If I was caught speeding—"

"No, no," he said. "This isn't about a ticket."

It was his voice, at once embarrassed and determined, that tipped me off. Of course he was calling about my father. Why else would a Princeton cop phone me. I got up and, pulling the door shut, stepped deeper into the closet.

"You're Shoichi Yoshikawa's daughter?" he asked.

"That's right."

I was already planning ahead. My father must have had another breakdown. He'd probably been found roaming the streets, clad in nothing but boxer shorts and raving about being cheated of the Nobel. Could one of my sisters take a train down tonight to check on him at the hospital and sign the forms? I'd leave early on Sunday, forget the post-wedding brunch.

If I thought for even one second that my father getting sick the day before my wedding was the universe punishing me for leaving him off the invite list, I'd manage to blot it out.

The rehearsal dinner, scheduled for that evening at the Isabella Stewart Gardner Museum, was black tie. Even aside from the missing earrings, I was a mess, in a tee and yoga pants, eyeliner smudged, hair slopping out of a ponytail. But I could probably make myself presentable in a half hour, which left enough time for most of the calls I'd need to make.

The cop said, "Shoichi Yoshikawa of Hartley Avenue, Princeton?"

In my half of the closet, shirts slipped off hangers; jeans spilled out of drawers. On Rob's side, gray and black sports coats stood at attention. I tugged at the sleeve of one, feeling the rasp of wool. "Yes," I said. "*Yes.* Is he okay?"

"No, ma'am," he said. "I'm sorry, but I need to inform you that your father died last night."

"That's not possible."

"The medical examiner believes he died of natural causes—"

"There must be a mistake," I said, but the words were automatic. Though just seventy-six, my father had a heart condition.

"I saw his body this morning, on his bed at home," the cop said. "The television was blasting."

Around me the world was constricting in a way that felt familiar. Had I really thought that marrying Rob would change anything—that I'd finally have some peace?

"I realize this must come as a shock." The cop was speaking now in a way that was clearly rehearsed. "But we want you to know that we believe it was a peaceful passing."

There was paperwork to fill out, he said. When could I come down to Princeton?

Although his voice was deep, he sounded young. When I met him three days later, he'd turn out to be ginger-haired, but otherwise exactly as I imagined: tall, gawky, big-nosed, and in his early thirties, new to the job but learning fast.

I wanted to explain. I wanted to tell him that I was forty-four and never planned to get hitched, that when Rob and I had finally decided to take the plunge I agonized over whether to invite my father, that I didn't want to put my mother and okay, fine, if you must, myself through the ordeal of having him at the wedding, that I'd gone back and forth on it for months before convincing myself that the person I was really sparing was *him*. It'd be mean, in fact downright cruel, to make my father watch my stepfather walk me down the aisle.

What I said instead was, "Tomorrow's my wedding day."

There was a silence, and then the cop did the only thing that made sense. He laughed.

◉

Rob was in the car with his brother, sister-in-law, and filmmaker friends from the Midwest, and when I called him I went straight to speaker. Upon hearing my voice, his friends and brother began shouting: they love me; it's not too late to back out; who's the lucky guy anyway? They were belting out Billy Idol when Rob picked up the phone.

"You all right?" he asked.

He sounded concerned. I'd been laughing, attempting to sing along with the others, and despite the years we'd been together I felt anew the miracle of it, how well he knew me.

"Keep this to yourself," I said. I told him and there was an intake of breath. But his voice was steady: he'd be home right away.

My mother and my stepfather, Jimmy, were in a downtown Boston café with my middle stepsister and her new baby. Four and a half hours remained before we were all due to show up at the rehearsal dinner. My mother hadn't even laid eyes on my father for more than twenty-five years, but perhaps there was no way to soften this particular blow. Still, I should have tried. I realized that even as I heard myself giving her the news straight.

"Daddy died this morning."

"What do you mean—"

I tried a number of different phrases. At last she uttered a cry, not loud but sharp.

A few minutes of muted back and forth. Then Jimmy came on the line, his voice heavy. "I'm really sorry, Mako. Are you okay?"

"Yes. But this weekend," I said. "The wedding. Everyone will be showing up soon. We need to decide whether to go ahead with it or cancel."

"I suppose that's right," Jimmy said. I could feel him gathering his thoughts. "Aren't there other options? You could make an announcement at the wedding. Something to honor his memory."

I hesitated.

"Shoichi was a great man," he said. "I know he wasn't always a great father, but his work was world-changing."

I rolled my eyes. Jimmy thought I undersold my father, I knew he hyped him up. But now wasn't the time to get into it. I hadn't considered an announcement. In my head I began drafting.

Missing today is someone who should—

Not to cast a pall, but—

I didn't invite my father this weekend, and now he—

"Can you start me off?" I said.

"Physics genius," Jimmy said. "Innovative, inspirational, acclaimed for his brilliance."

Asylum inmate. Violent, vicious, convinced he was God reincarnate.

"Celebrated world leader in fusion energy research," he said. "Maybe something about groundbreaking—"

Would-be world leader. Nobel Prize noncontender. Groundbreaker who broke.

In the background the baby gurgled. I could hear my stepsister pitching questions, my mother lobbing back answers in short, murmured bursts.

I imagined standing at the podium in the grand ballroom of the Ritz, where the reception would be, the chandeliers and the tables laden with flowers and glasses and fancy plates. I wouldn't use Jimmy's hyperbole, but I'd give my father his due. *A noted physicist. Dedicated his life to one of the world's most pressing problems.* The guests in their finery would blink. Their smiles would go slack, the flutes they'd reflexively reached for freezing in midair. Were they there to celebrate or mourn? To congratulate or condole, to mark a joining of two lives or the passing of another?

And me gussied up in white, when I should be in black.

"I think we have to cancel," I said. "Don't you?"

Jimmy sighed. "It's your decision," he said. "Just let us know."

"Is Mom up for talking?"

When I asked her how she was, she said the more important question was if I was all right, and how was I feeling about the wedding?

"We should call it off," I said.

An inward breath. "But everyone's here. That doesn't seem—"

Jimmy said something I couldn't make out. My mother replied, her voice also muffled—she must have covered the phone's mouthpiece—and then Jimmy spoke again.

I should have known she wouldn't want to cancel. She'd been excited about the wedding, and from decades of practice, she was unrivaled at compartmentalizing.

But I was surprised. She'd loved him for years. A part of her did still.

Then my mother was back. "Whatever you decide," she said, sounding resigned. "You know what's best."

Did I?

I was a wedding cautionary tale. Daydreaming about disinviting Mom or Dad, prospective brides and grooms would think of me and shudder.

Forty-five minutes later, Rob's filmmaking friends were with my grad-school ones in our kitchen, and his long arms were wrapped around me on our bed.

I was gathering myself to ask about the wedding when he spoke. "I'm so sorry," he said.

I drew back. His own father had died just a year and a half ago, a loss Rob was still grieving.

"My dad wasn't like yours," I said. "You know that."

He didn't flinch. "I do," he said. "I was actually talking about the timing. Today of all days."

His eyes—large and expressive, set in a face that's all angles—were steady. Guileless. Was he telling the truth, or just saving face? Maybe he'd offered solace only to realize he had to pivot, and fast.

On one hand, I was bristling. Did Rob think me heartless? How dare he, when he knew so little about my father. On the other, I felt wary. If he did know the whole sad story, might he think me damaged?

And on the other other hand, there was guilt, laced with shame. I should have told him the story years ago. God knows I'd meant to.

But maybe I was being too hard on myself. The broad outlines I'd provided about my father, cruel/crazy/violent and now estranged, weren't untrue.

I propped my chin on his chest. "So what about the wedding?"

"Up to you," he said. "We can go ahead with it or postpone—because that's what we'd be doing, *cancel* is the wrong term. What Jimmy said, making an announcement at the beginning, that's not my top choice." His lips quirked. "Talk about buzzkill."

Wedding paraphernalia was strewn around the room. The three bowties, gray grayer grayest, that Rob had been trying to choose among and that I couldn't tell apart. The elegant high-heeled shoes I loved and the ones I could actually dance in. The four boxes of party headgear that we'd hoped, through a plan still TBD, to distribute and persuade all the guests to wear: head boppers, antennae made up of feather tufts and disco balls, and an assortment of ears—bunny, bear, Mickey Mouse, leopard, tiger, and my choice, spangled black cat. Slanted jauntily atop my dancing shoes was Rob's pick, one-of-a-kind scarlet devil's horns.

"Let's do it," I said.

"Really?"

I ticked the reasons off. The out-of-town guests already in or on their way to Boston. The (nonrefundable) cost of the Gardner and the Ritz. The impossibility of doing this again, on this scale and with all these friends and relatives from faraway.

"Even so, I can't help feeling a bit queasy about it," I said. "Going through with the wedding seems—well, like a lie. A kind of betrayal."

Rob nodded. "I feel like that, too."

"A betrayal of our guests, I mean," I added quickly. "Keeping something so big a secret."

Another nod. Had he not thought I meant a betrayal of my father—was that just me?

Rob was unshaved, and he'd want a shower. To get ready, we needed an hour, maybe more.

"Another sticking point is the karma question," I said. "Do we want to start out our married life like this. But I'm not too worried about that."

He was watching me. "Me neither."

"Then we're—"

"The issue for me," he cut in, "is whether you're up for this, in a way that's more than just smiling for the guests and parroting vows."

There it was, the difference between us. For Rob the wedding was about commitment. The ceremony was the point. To me, the wedding was a bash. A big one, to be sure, a once-in-a-lifetime chance to bring together far-flung relatives and friends, and one that involved pageantry—but in the end, just a party.

"The question," he said, "is if you can set this all aside and be genuine—genuinely have fun and get married."

It was a fair question. An approximation of fun was within my grasp, I felt sure of that. *Genuinely* was a tall order, but I'd do my best.

No. The answer to his question was no.

I smiled at him. "Let's get dressed."

◉

We were late to the Gardner.

Along with the donning of party wear, there'd been more calls: my father's girlfriend, sobbing and barely coherent; our wedding planner, for a final check-in; my older sister, who'd gasped, rallied, and said she'd let our younger sister know; the Princeton cop and our father's lawyer, to arrange when we'd meet on Monday; two wedding guests who were lost/late. Afterward, more deliberations between Rob and me: do we tell anyone else and if so, who, what, how, and when? The arrival of my best friend, who sat on the bed and held me as I cried. The drive through the heavy rain. The turn I missed in the maze of traffic that was Storrow.

But once Rob and I were inside the Gardner entryway, stomping our feet, shaking umbrellas, and peeling off coats, I felt different. For hours I hadn't been thinking of the rehearsal dinner except as the easier part of the weekend to get through: only forty guests, mostly family and good friends, with little for Rob and me to do other than welcome people, make small talk, consume our dinner, and look amused/comically rueful/touched at the right moments in the toasts. So it was a revelation to stand in the entryway, somber and magisterial, and see the glowing lights and the green of the ferns and palm trees of the Italian palazzo courtyard ahead, and hear the buzz of a festive crowd and a string quartet playing Vivaldi. As our eyes adjusted, Rob and I could make out heads swiveling in our direction, faces breaking out in wide smiles, and then we were being kissed, hugged, clapped on the back and congratulated, glasses of wine and puff pastry concoctions materializing in our hands, and then Rob was plunging into the crowd, showering greetings and jokes and introductions, laughter and warmth lapping in his wake.

The weekend would be fine—better than fine. Tonight we'd dine here, in one of the great houses of the world, to the soft strains of violins; tomorrow Rob and I would tie the knot before a hundred guests; and on Sunday morning I'd wake up early, make my apologies to those staying at our house, and power down the turnpike with my sisters to Princeton, where we'd lay our father's body to rest.

Rob and I were waiting, our bossy photographer having finally corralled us, when he told me that my younger sister had been crying.

"Fuck," I said. I'd seen her, but I'd been with others and across the room, and when I looked over again, she was gone. Lost in the crush of the crowd, I'd assumed, but I realized now she'd been hiding from me. I bit my lip. "You talked to her?"

Handsome in his suit, his face clean-shaven, he nodded. "She was really upset."

His gaze was on the courtyard's ceiling, the tops of its Doric columns. I could feel his tension, his confusion and yearning to understand.

"Forget the photos," I said. "Let's run."

Grabbing glasses of wine, we fled up the stairs. The second floor was empty; an hour into the party, most of the guests had already made the trek to those galleries and now wanted to stay near each other and the kind waiters with their trays of delicacies and drinks. Hand in hand, our heels echoing on the marble floors, Rob and I wandered through the rooms crammed with art and decorated to an inch of their lives, and in spite of everything, I knew I'd treasure the memory of this solitary nighttime jaunt.

We paused in the stolen Vermeer room. I wanted to make excuses for my sister, which seemed all too easy. Obviously she was exhausted and not herself—five months pregnant, and just off a big business trip and a flight from China!

"I guess the news hit her hard," I said.

"She was barely holding it together." Rob was peering at a tapestry on the wall.

I kept my eyes on it, too. "She must be so pissed."

I felt rather than saw his eyes slide toward me. "She just seemed sad."

"Give her time."

I was imagining her putting on her party dress, applying mascara on streaming eyes, outlining her lips with shaking hands. Greeting family friends, forcing a smile, parrying questions and party chitchat from well-meaning strangers, when all she wanted was to be alone and remember our father and cry.

"I put her in an impossible situation," I said.

"I didn't know she and your dad were close," Rob said, his gaze back on the tapestry.

"She never lived with him, not the way the rest of us did. When we left, she was eight. Too young to remember much. And it's not like she's seen much of him since then."

It wasn't enough. I could feel Rob waiting.

"She wasn't close to him," I said, "at least not exactly, but she's also not—" Hardened by years of hate and anger. Determined not to grieve. Relieved that he's gone.

"—like me," I said.

"You sure you're not upset?" he said. "His death won't hit you later?"

I turned, ready to snap, only to soften when confronted by his gaze. He was worried about me, and in all fairness, his questions were ones I needed to consider—and I would. Just not right now.

"I'm not my sister," I said, taking him by the arm. "I knew our father. She never did."

The dinner had been delicious, the toasts filled with the usual jokes and dubious insights about marriage and the bride and groom, and the night was winding down. My mother might be the champ compartmentalizer, but trained at her feet, I was no slouch, and I was laughing with two of Rob's cousins, the thought of my father's death locked away so securely it was almost not there, when I caught sight of a longtime family friend. The widow of a fusion colleague of my father's, she was standing alone and watching me.

Our eyes met, and I knew.

I excused myself to the cousins.

The widow had been something of a guardian angel to my mother during the hard, lonely years after we'd left my father's house. She'd always been kind to me, but she and I weren't close. At the start of the evening, she and I had exchanged pleasantries, nothing more.

I leaned against the wall beside her and together we gazed out at the party.

"So you heard," I said.

"News travels fast in the lab circle."

"I remember it as a tight group."

"A lot has changed," she said. "But yes, many of us in the old guard, we stay in touch."

Off to the left, my mother was luminous, chatting away as a group of Rob's friends huddled around her, smiling. In a long velvet dress, her Louise Brooks bob framing her face, she looked effortlessly at ease, a seamless fit with the elegant surroundings.

Leaning against the wall, the widow and I watched her.

"She's doing well, isn't she?" the widow said at last.

"There's her health, of course. But yes, not bad."

"You look like her."

Throughout the evening, I'd been hearing versions of that from family friends: *your mother's daughter.* It was a phrase I always liked to hear, but tonight it felt particularly welcome.

"I remember when your father first came to the lab," the widow said. "How proud she was of him. Not that that was a surprise. He was like a blaze. So brilliant, and so warmhearted."

People who knew my father tended to hew to a script. Awe at

his gifts followed by a sigh. The phrase *What a shame* coded or left unsaid because why bother, it was already in everyone's minds.

Warmhearted: that was off script.

"Back then," the widow said, "the lab was like a family."

All at once I felt ashamed. She'd seen me laughing. The food and backdrop were so lavish. "This weekend," I said. "The wedding. I didn't—"

Her hand was on my arm. "Don't," she said, her voice low but clear. "I get it. We all do."

She was so close I could hear the faint jangle of her earrings. I focused on the sound and willed myself not to cry.

"Your father—" She shook her head. "No one blames you."

At the end of the night, driving home with a carload of guests, I was furious with myself. Enough with the self-pity and drama. The universe wasn't conspiring against me. My father didn't die out of spite. Even worse, in my self-absorption I'd nearly missed the real lesson here: my father was and always would be part of my life. I couldn't change that, and shouldn't try.

It was a lesson I needed to learn.

Why, after all, had my heart been so set on Jimmy walking me down the aisle, when I'd never much liked the idea of the father "giving away" the bride, one man ceding possession of her to the next? It was obvious. I wanted to be seen and known as Jimmy's and my mother's daughter.

The wedding had never been *just a party*. Without knowing it, I'd been thinking of it all along as a junction, a crossing into a world in which my father had never been.

Almost immediately after buying our moldering modern masterpiece of a house half a year back, Rob and I had resolved to get married in it, beneath the thirty-foot-tall ficus tree that grew in the atrium. What better way to make the house ours, we said, bullish despite the contractors' warnings. On the day of our wedding, the varnish was still tacky, but if we kept the lights low, the house was presentable, and the night before we'd conscripted our houseguests into staying up late and helping us staple a head bopper to the bottom of each of our hundred-plus rental chairs, which we'd then set up, angling them until they more or less fit into the still-unfurnished atrium.

Rob and I got dressed together, wedding superstitions be damned. We'd run out our bad luck, and I needed someone to airlift and then strap me into the dress, which was a feat of human ingenuity, engineering, and architecture, its skirt airy and so immense I'd need help to pee. With only a tinge of regret, I slipped on the shoes I could dance in. Rob slid into his tux, so dark and smooth it looked slick.

At last we were ready. Below, the classical guitarist was playing the Beatles, which meant that guests had been seated and were beginning to quiet. I could hear Jimmy, who'd already knocked on our door twice to hurry us along, calling up to say that it was time.

"Great choice," I said, nodding at Rob's bowtie, and then he and I fist-bumped and descended the stairs hand in hand.

I was coming apart. Perhaps it was the conversation with the widow, perhaps just the shock wearing off, the news starting to sink in. I'd wept the night before, stifling my sobs in my pillow, and then again in the morning.

At least I hadn't woken Rob. At least he was grinning now, joining in with the guitar to serenade me with "In My Life."

Then Jimmy was walking me down our makeshift aisle. Poems were read; my middle stepsister wrapped us in a blanket she'd made; Rob broke a glass. At the minister's request, everyone put on the headgear they found under their chairs, and with the head boppers bopping and the animal ears pricking up in our direction, Rob and I said our vows and exchanged rings. Then the caravan in cars and a mega-bus to the Ritz, where there were more toasts and dinner, and Rob and I did the dance we'd rehearsed for weeks.

Throughout, my younger sister kept out of sight. I was twirling with guests on the dance floor when I finally spied her. She was sitting with a group of others, but even from the dance floor I could see that her eyes were red-rimmed, her lips a line. I admitted it to myself then. I'd lied to Rob. I didn't know our father any better than she did. Maybe he deserved the tears she'd shed for him. Maybe he changed; in the end, maybe there was good in him. Hell, he might even have been as warmhearted as the widow said—yes, that, too, was possible.

For most of my life I'd thought that my father's unhappiness was rooted in his professional failures and disappointments. It was the story he believed, and I saw no reason to question it. Only recently had I come to suspect that his bitterness had another source. He was so alone: alienated from his kin in Japan, all but friendless, barely in touch with his daughters. He'd been adored by wives, lovers, and girlfriends—even, once upon a time, by me. But if being with Rob had taught me anything, it was that loving others was the gift. That was great fortune and success.

Had my father ever loved anyone? I doubted it, but the truth was I didn't know.

My eyes were stinging. Even if I'd managed not to spoil the day, Rob's wish that I genuinely have fun—what a spectacular botch. In the end, though, what was a wedding if not a threshold for two, a transition to a new union? I made a vow then. I'd take joy in our marriage for all our years to come.

As if the thought conjured him, there was Rob on the dance floor. James Brown was urging us to get on up, and he was heeding his call, stutter-stepping toward me as his hands lifted over his head in his signature move, pushing the ceiling to the left and then the right. As my ridiculous skirt swung out, I reached for him, our bodies moving in time.

FAVORITE STORY

When I was four, I used to ride on his shoulders while clutching his hair, black and bristly as an ink brush. It must have hurt, but he never complained. He swung me in an arc in our backyard, and I shrieked with laughter.

When I was ten, he introduced me to Isaac Asimov. We spent the summer reading and rereading matching copies of *I, Robot* on the couch together, the whisky in his glass holding the light of the afternoon sun.

When I asked, at the old-enough-to-know-better age of eleven, if Elvis Presley died of old age, he burst out laughing. I didn't realize it then, but he was forty-two, the exact same age as the King at his death. This became his favorite story, and he'd tell it again and again over the years, until eventually I laughed, too.

When I received my long-delayed doctorate, he sent a congratulatory note: *Another Dr. Yoshikawa!* When I published my first novel at thirty-three, he bought all four copies at the local bookstore. *The cashier couldn't believe you were my daughter.*

MY FATHER'S WOMEN

When I drove my sisters back to town from the lawyer's office three days after our father's death, it took a while for us to arrive at the subject of his women. The lawyer had run us through the will—no surprises, 20 percent to each of us, a little more to his final companion, and a little less to his two stepdaughters from his second marriage. We knew that his estate, which included a parking lot in a commercial district in Tokyo as well as a summerhouse near Mount Fuji, was considerable. Yet none of us had any idea where the right documents were, and for some time our conversation lurched from where to look for them to what kind of service to hold to how to clear the house of its clutter to when to see the body and how best to lay it to rest.

At last we grew quiet. We were tired, still jolted from the call that had yanked us back to this town.

My older sister broke the silence. "Out of all those girlfriends and wives," she said, "out of all the women he had, who did he love the most?"

I glanced at her. Overcome by the shock, she'd cried at the lawyer's, but she looked composed enough now.

My younger sister said Ellie, hands down. His second wife, the love of his middle age, his partner in bowling and church dinners. She reminded us of the episode he'd had after her death and the long hospitalization that had followed. "That was a bad one, even for him."

I shook my head. "That's just because her death came out of nowhere. Don't you remember how he used to goad her about God?"

Rousing herself, my older sister nodded. "He'd point out all the places the Bible contradicted itself."

"And all the ways God was a logical impossibility."

"She'd get so mad she couldn't speak."

"Besides," I said, "since when did any of his episodes occur for a reason?" It was obvious: he was happiest with Toshiko-san, his last companion. So what if she hadn't gone to college? Our father, Shoichi Yoshikawa, had been a Princeton University physicist and a prominent fusion energy researcher. None of his women—a category that included us, Ivy League graduates all—understood physics on his level; few in the world did. Toshiko-san had made him laugh, no mean feat, and they'd had Japan, not to mention the food, culture, and language, in common.

"But if he loved her so much," my younger sister shot back, "why didn't he marry her?"

To which I had no answer.

We were in our late thirties and forties. It had taken a while, but with me finally married, all three of us were partnered off. We'd grown up in Princeton and left it as soon as we could, the two of them hightailing it to California. I stayed in the northeast, but in the last two decades I'd seen our father as seldom as they, my neglect rendered more glaring by my proximity and the fact that I, a child-less novelist and professor, had more time to spare.

Systematically we went down the list of the women who'd passed through Shoichi's life: girlfriends whose names we could barely recall, drinking partners, one or two con women who were after his bank account or citizenship papers or simply the cash in his wallet. But we dismissed those as infatuations. Of course none of us suggested his first wife, our mother.

My older sister had fallen silent, her eyes fastened on the landscape, at once familiar and strange, whipping by outside the window.

I pulled to a stop at a traffic light. "You okay?"

Her head still averted, she said, "Do you ever wonder—"

Her voice was husky. By coincidence, we'd all visited him, though at different times, this past spring, but before that none of us had seen him for years.

She cleared her throat. "Do you think it's possible that he never loved any of them?"

Behind us my younger sister released a breath. I gazed ahead. The sky was overcast, but the trees along the road were rinsed with fall color.

Then the light changed to green, I pressed on the accelerator, and my older sister turned from the window and asked where we should stop for lunch.

He was born in Tokyo, the scion of a wealthy family descended from samurai. His parents, grandparents, and nursemaids doted on him. On his fifth birthday, his mother died of pneumonia. Less than two years later, World War II began. Food was scarce during the war years, and Shoichi almost starved, his stomach bloating.

By the Occupation, his life was back on track. He'd acquired a stepmother; soon he had two much younger half siblings who looked up to him. He became interested in stamps, and at the age of eleven began traveling across Japan on his own to find and collect them.

He was a striking teenager, tall with a shock of black hair and enormous, arresting eyes. His grin was sudden and bright and took up his face. A star student, he attended the University of Tokyo for his undergraduate degree and MIT for his doctorate. After MIT he took a job on a temporary basis at Princeton University. Except for a two-year stint as a professor at the University of Tokyo, he ended up staying at Princeton for forty years, through increasingly severe bipolar episodes and breaks with reality, bouts of rage and violence, a slide into alcoholism, and a long string of professional failures.

My sisters and I held his memorial service in a small room at the local Hyatt. We'd looked into using the university chapel, with its stained glass windows and soaring ceilings, and had been secretly relieved to find that it was booked for holiday festivities through December. The chapel, which seats two thousand, would have echoed even more than usual with only a handful of mourners in attendance.

In the end more than fifty people came, so many that we had to scramble for more chairs. My mother's old gang of Japanese women friends was there, as well as Ellie's daughters and their families. The rest were scientists: the neighbors, a group that sported two Nobel winners, and a few friends my father had acquired since retirement through MIT's alumni association. It was the turnout from the lab, which numbered more than two dozen, that had thrown off our count.

At the memorial, one of the last speakers said that Shoichi used to ask his women to make dishes for their church dinners. "Because," she added, drawling, "of course he always had a woman."

I winced. The audience laughed, but the remark seemed in poor taste, given that Toshiko-san was in the room—in the back row, where she'd insisted on placing herself.

The service had been stocked with surprises, one or two even more startling than the fact that my father had continued the practice, initiated by Ellie, of attending church dinners. There was the letter, translated and read out loud by my older sister, from an old high-school friend in Tokyo. Some of what was in the letter was familiar—accounts of Shoichi's effortless brilliance, for instance. But much of it was new. I didn't know that in high school he was popular with boys and girls alike, and friendly and generous to those less favored than himself. For as long as I could remember, he'd been a poor conversationalist, an aggressive and mean-spirited debater, and a teller of boastful, embarrassing stories, the kind of person people avoided at parties and dreaded bumping into in the street. I didn't know that he always came in last in the 100-meter dash or that his genial indifference to his lack of athleticism somehow added to his popularity and his aura of cool. I didn't even know that he still kept in touch with anyone from high school—sixty years ago!—let alone a man who would weep at his passing, write such a letter, and then round up every single graduate of their high school he could find so they could hold a memorial service of their own in Tokyo.

Another surprise was the picture that emerged of Shoichi as a teacher and mentor. One after the next, his colleagues and former students spoke with wistfulness of the same heady time: the sixties and seventies, when their lab, the premier center for fusion research in the world, overflowed with bright young men fired up by the conviction that the discovery of a clean energy source lay within their grasp. And how could they not have faith, they said, with Shoichi at the helm? They spoke of traveling across the country to study with him, basking in his presence, and angling for invitations to dinner at his home—of trusting that his genius and leadership would win the day for them, the lab, and mankind.

The image of adoring students and colleagues clustering around my father clashed with what I remembered. If my mother hadn't said later that her memories of those times matched the speakers' exactly, I would have assumed they'd made it up. Shoichi lived just a few miles from the lab, but by the end, most of his colleagues hadn't seen him for years. With each breakdown and hospitalization, their friendship with him had cooled, and when he retired ten years ago, it must have seemed easier to forget him. I couldn't blame them. By then illness, medication, and electroshock treatments had done their damage. His mind was diminished and his body bloated. His hands shook, and his gaze was restless but no longer searching.

I wondered at first if the speakers were waxing nostalgic about Shoichi to compensate for their neglect. But then I realized that they, too, had been disappointed by their careers. They weren't famous. None of them had won the Nobel. Their nostalgia wasn't for Shoichi so much as for those heady days at the lab, when their ambition and their idealism had run side by side and success seemed around the corner. Or if the nostalgia was for him, it was for the man he had been, as well as for their own younger selves.

The fact that my father had "always had a woman" wasn't a surprise. He liked the company of women, the more the merrier. Toshiko-san knew it, and probably many in the room did as well. He was so crude and boastful it was difficult not to know.

"Toshiko-san is the primary mourner here," my older sister said in her opening remarks, "no question." More than once I turned around to search for her, a trim, plainly dressed woman with an open face, fighting tears by herself in the back. But the room was too packed. I couldn't see past the fourth row.

Despite my sister's words, at the reception afterward it was to us, the daughters, that the guests came to pay their respects, never mind that we hadn't been involved in our father's life in any serious way for years. Toshiko-san probably received fewer expressions of sympathy than our mother, who'd flown in from England to attend the service.

Toshiko-san and my father had met ten years earlier, after being introduced by the sushi chef at their favorite restaurant. Soon afterward she moved in with him, but without ever giving up her own apartment, and for reasons that weren't clear to me, she moved back into her own place after the first couple of years. He took her on trips to Japan, Europe, and Canada and on cruises to beaches in sunnier climes. They ended their relationship more than once but always found their way back to each other. When I came to visit, they would take me to the restaurant where they'd met. We'd share large boats of sushi. She would have too many beers and clamber to the front of the room to sing karaoke, mostly sappy songs, Christopher Cross and the like, her voice wavering in and out of tune, as my father watched and smiled, nodding his head ever so slightly to the beat.

She never called him by name. Instead she used the term *sensei*, an honorific title meaning "professor"—a sign of respect, maybe, or a joke, a way to gently mock him and bring him down to earth. I was grateful for it, since it made him laugh.

In the last two years of his life, he and Toshiko-san saw each other only once a week. They met every Friday for about an hour at a mall on Route 1 that stood almost exactly between their homes. Yet even if they saw little of each other, they talked. Toshiko-san told me after his death that he'd call her twice a day, at nine in the morning and nine at night. She didn't have to explain the reason for this ritual. A caricature of the absent-minded scientist, Shoichi was oblivious to the progress of the clock. If he insisted on such precise times, it was because he was worried about his body lying there, undiscovered, for hours or even days.

As it was, the funeral home director said that based on the decomposition of his body, a full day must have passed before he was discovered. Shoichi hadn't phoned at night, but since that had happened before, Toshiko-san decided to wait for the morning call. When that didn't come, she peeled down Route 1 in her old Toyota putt putt, gripping the wheel all the way.

She banged on the door and then ran around tapping on all the windows. She had the key but was too frightened to use it. She went to our nearest neighbors, an astrophysicist and his wife. They'd lived next door to my father for decades and were used to helping out; the last time my father was found ranting in the backyard, clad in nothing but boxer shorts on a frigid February day, it was the astrophysicist who called me. When Toshiko-san asked him for help, his son was visiting, and it was with him that she'd gone inside to find Shoichi dead on his bed, the television blasting.

Five days later, my sisters and I assembled with Toshiko-san at the funeral home for a viewing of the body. Shoichi had requested a cremation. The viewing was just for the four of us.

He was dressed in a gray suit. His face looked sunken. The room was cold and dimly lit.

Toshiko-san was muttering. "Look like he's sleeping, *ne.*" She was rocking back and forth, her eyes streaming. "Wake up, *sensei.* Wake up. *Itsumo nebo.*" *Always a sleepyhead.* "Look at him, so handsome in his suit."

She turned to us, and we—huddled silently together in a corner, my younger sister red-eyed—gaped back.

"You see how handsome he is?" she said. Turning back to the body, she swiped at her eyes. "What'll I do without you, *ne, sensei?* Who's gonna take me on nice cruises?" Reaching into the coffin, she pushed on his shoulder with two fingers, hard enough to leave a dent. "*Wake up.*"

When Rob and I were clearing out my father's house and Toshiko-san came over to help, she immediately set to work. Though he'd cross-dressed when I was young, I didn't know if my father had worn the dresses, skirts, and nightgowns that were jam-packed in his closets and drawers, but Toshiko-san sure seemed eager to throw them away. Hours passed before I could coax her to sit for a cup of tea.

When I asked her about her childhood in Japan, at first she said little. Dazed by grief, I thought, until she glanced up to fix me with a look. In October, she said, a few weeks before his death, she and *sensei* had driven right past Boston on one of their trips. "I said why not call Mako-san. He say no."

I reeled back. Although the comment seemed designed to hurt, her expression was quizzical, and devoid of spite. Yet her words did wound. The thought of her urging my father to phone me and him being too hurt, or was that too proud, to try again—because he *had* called, he'd left me a voicemail the week before their trip—was all but unbearable.

But I needed to ask her about him.

"He must have wanted to focus on you," I said, trying for lightness.

When she didn't reply, I went back to asking about Japan. Feeling unburdened, maybe, she began to relax, and after a while she was laughing and doing voices and I was hearing about her childhood amid the temples and shrines in Kyoto; the work she did for her parents' kimono dyeing business, lugging vats of water and churning the heavy cloth; and her six sisters and one brother, the youngest, who inherited the family business and promptly ran it into the ground. She talked about the handsome young Black soldier who wooed her with chocolates and spirited her across an ocean. *He wanted a souvenir from Japan. He got me.*

Listening, I felt more certain. My father's relationship with her hadn't been one-sided. In the wake of Ellie's death, he'd been softer and needier, newly appreciative of having someone loving around.

I had it planned. My plan was to toss a softball—in what ways was *sensei* kind?—before ramping up to tougher questions.

Yet when she paused to drain her cup, I found myself on a different tack.

"Did my father ever hit you?"

The question didn't seem to surprise her. "No."

"Do you think he hit Ellie?"

She nodded, the light glinting off her bifocals. "Maybe," she said. "Maybe that *why* he never hit me."

"So that wasn't why you moved out of his house."

She shook her head, expressionless.

Maybe it was the combination of my father's death and my own very recent wedding; the fact that I was in my father's kitchen, the site of some of my worst memories; or Toshiko-san herself. But I found myself saying something I'd rarely voiced.

"He hit my mother. A lot. And my older sister and me."

"Japanese men," Toshiko-san said.

We looked at each other. I said, "Are American men all that different?"

In the months to come, Toshiko-san would tell me how her husband, a teetotaler when she met him, began drinking heavily back in America, maybe because of the pain from a war injury, and how when he was drunk, he beat her. She'd tell me how she moved out though they never divorced, and how, almost a decade later, when he lay dying of cancer, she moved back to nurse and take care of him. But that afternoon, so early in our friendship, all she said was, "American men, too. American men, too."

"So why did you move out?" I asked.

"A woman from Russia. She clean his house. If you want be friends with her, I say, I go home."

"What did he say?" I asked, already guessing the answer.

Toshiko-san wore a smile. Her bifocals hid her eyes. "Your father, he women crazy, *ne.*"

When she and Shoichi met at the mall on Route 1, they'd stroll, look into store windows, and chat. Sometimes they had lunch or a snack, but this was never the primary purpose of the visit. She'd reminisce about events from her past as well as theirs, catch him up on her children, grandchildren, and great-grandchildren, and scold him for scrounging at flea markets and accumulating yet more clutter. He'd ask a question or toss in a remark here or there; at times he threw his head back and laughed, something he did rarely in the last few years of his life, and then only with her. He had little news to impart of his only grandchild, whom he'd met just a few times; in his last decade he and my older sister were seldom in touch. But I like to think that at times during those weekly walks he broke his customary silence to speculate about his granddaughter and that Toshiko-san wondered with him. Did she still play with stuffed animals? Had she mastered fractions yet? How tall had she grown?

An Asian man and an Asian woman, stooped and gray-haired, their conversation slipping from Japanese to English and then back again: anyone seeing them would have taken them for a long-married couple, out shopping for a toy for a grandchild.

Toshiko-san loved my father. But my younger sister was right—his feelings for her were open to question. He'd been resolute in his refusal to marry her. Once I asked him about it, and he reminded me that she was seven years older than he was. He didn't want to bury another wife. Ellie's death, from complications resulting from diabetes, had been too hard. He couldn't go through that again.

I pointed out that Toshiko-san was in great health and that women usually outlived men. And besides, isn't it better to live for the moment? Was there something else he wasn't telling me?

It made no difference what I said. He wouldn't change his mind, nor would he explain further.

So perhaps he hadn't loved her—but there might have been someone else, someone he'd cherished and lost.

At the end of the memorial service, one of his MIT friends had come up to me. He said that in the weeks leading up to his death, Shoichi had told him that being bipolar had ruined his life. I hadn't been able to collect myself enough to respond, and the man ran off before I could find out his name, so I couldn't call to ask him which aspects of his life my father had meant. His career, I had to assume—yet I couldn't help wondering now if he'd meant something more.

That my father hadn't fulfilled the academic promise of his early years—that he, unlike the nuclear physicist next door, wasn't summoned to Sweden to dance with the queen and receive the Nobel—was old news. I'd made my peace with that disappointment long ago, even if he never could. But the idea that love also eluded him was new, and harder to accept.

It was getting married myself, of course, that was propelling this line of thought. Fresh from exchanging vows, I wanted to believe that my father had loved someone, someone he'd been happy with at least for a while. Struggling with my third novel, I'd sought refuge in Rob's company as well as that of my mother and friends. Had my father had recourse to this solace?

The thought of him truly caring for someone seemed improbable—it *was* improbable. But not impossible.

Over the years I'd grilled my father's psychiatrists, internists, and nurses and read clinical texts, scientific papers, and memoirs and novels about bipolar disorder. I knew about the controversies surrounding its diagnosis, the difficulty of understanding how exactly it affects the brain, and the many problems associated with lithium, the most reliable medication currently available. I knew that alcoholism was a symptom, that travel can trigger a manic episode, that studies link the illness with creativity and that it runs in families. I knew that it could make people say and do things they didn't mean and hurt themselves as well as anyone else in their vicinity. I knew how others with bipolar disorder had fared: how Van Gogh walked to a wheat field he'd been painting to shoot himself in the chest; how Woolf weighted her pockets with stones and waded into the Ouse;

how Hemingway pushed the barrel of a shotgun into his mouth and pulled the trigger; how Plath sealed off her children's bedroom door before sticking her head in the oven; how both Rothko and Diane Arbus took a slug of barbiturates and sawed their veins with razors; how Anne Sexton wrapped herself in her mother's old fur coat, closed the garage and revved up her car; how Kurt Cobain skipped out on rehab and, after hiding out for days, returned to his garage to point his gun into his chin; how Spalding Gray jumped off the Staten Island Ferry into the East River; how David Foster Wallace knotted a rope around his neck on his patio; and how Alexander McQueen, taking no chances, overdosed on cocaine and tranquilizers, slashed his wrists, and hanged himself in his wardrobe using his favorite brown belt.

Yet nowhere had I heard that people with depression can't love. On the contrary, I knew from the work of the writer and psychologist Andrew Solomon that even though those with depression might feel temporarily unable to think about others, "in good spirits, some love themselves and some love others and some love work and some love God."

Who had my father loved? Surely the answer wasn't—it couldn't be—no one. It was odd. The thought gave me a chill.

So I wrote to Ellie's younger daughter. We'd gone to high school together, and though I hadn't seen her for years, we'd reconnected at the memorial service. I asked if she thought that my father had loved her mother. I begged her not to sugarcoat. What I wanted, I told her, was the truth.

Yes, she wrote back. *I think he did love her. With men, it's sometimes hard to separate love from pride, and I think he was very proud to have her as a wife.* They'd fought a lot, she said, especially over money, but they enjoyed their church community and loved their trips to Japan. *He was not a simple man and, consequently, a simple happiness was not in his nature,* she concluded, *but I did know him to have moments of simple pleasure and obvious joy.*

She was trying to reassure me, that was clear. But there was truth in what she said. My father had been proud of Ellie. He admired large, fleshy women—a hangover, I always thought, from the near starvation he had suffered as a boy in wartime Japan—and Ellie had been huge, her flesh spilling out of the bright sequined dresses she favored. Her calves were spindly and in her pumps she seemed immune to gravity, a parade float come to life. And she was a White woman: for a Japanese immigrant such as my father, perhaps a prize.

I'd forgotten that he and Ellie had argued about money as well as God, but maybe the good times outweighed the bad. Maybe pride did equal love.

But I didn't believe it.

I called my younger sister in San Jose.

"You said you thought he loved Ellie more than anyone else," I said. "Why?"

For a moment she was quiet. Then she laughed. "Process of elimination." Although still in mourning for our father, she was also seven months pregnant, glowing and huge, and her laugh sounded happy. She doesn't look much like our father—none of us do—but she has his grin, sudden and bright. "Think about it. Who else is there?"

"Oh," I said. "Oh. I thought that maybe you knew something about them. Maybe from when you went on vacation with them, at the beach."

"I remember—" She stopped.

I pictured her eyes growing distant, as they do when she guards her thoughts.

It took some prodding, but eventually she told me about a fight she'd overheard them having, just a few months after their wedding.

From what she could gather, Ellie had been trying to get him to pay for a credit card bill. He had told her that since she, as his wife, was now on his health plan, with all of her diabetes-related expenses covered, she had no right to expect anything more. "It went on," my sister said, "but that was the gist of it. So I'd say that the marriage probably sucked—though maybe less than his other relationships."

"Maybe things changed," I said, knowing, even as I spoke, that they hadn't. "They had ten more years together after that. That's a lot of time."

"Maybe. But it was a bad fight." She paused. "Listening to it, I thought about what you'd told me about the fights he and Mom used to have, and I was glad I didn't remember much about them."

It was with scant hope that I turned to the only candidate left. My mother, an artist and writer, was hard at work on her eighth book, an account based on interviews she'd conducted with Japanese veterans of World War II. In this and everything else, she had the unflagging support of Jimmy, a smart, well-read business executive she'd been married to for over twenty years. When Rob and I went to visit them over New Year's, I went to see her in her study. When I asked her to tell me about her relationship with my father, she nodded as if she'd been waiting for the question. The story unfurled slowly.

"I could see he was special," she said, "the day he showed up on our doorstep." He was eighteen, she two years younger, and he'd come to call on her parents at their summer home near the mountains of Karuizawa. He was stamp collecting in the area, and since his mother had been a relative of her father's, he decided on impulse to pay them a visit—so what if they had no idea who he was? He carried himself with the swagger of a Tokyo boy but was polite, personable, and well-spoken—"Yes, that really was your father back then," my mother said, though I hadn't stirred—and her parents were much taken with him. He spoke only with them, as if he were an adult, but she hid behind the shoji and eavesdropped, hearing enough to be impressed.

In the fall he traveled from Tokyo to Nagoya to have dinner at her family's home. By winter he was a regular guest. His looks and Tokyo sophistication dazzled her, but she already prized intellectual ability above all else, and it was to his brilliance she lost her heart. They struck up a correspondence, their relationship progressed, and she came to think their future together was assured.

But Shoichi held back. Maybe, my mother said, because of a girl he still liked from high school. Then one day he wrote to say he would marry her only if she promised always to obey him. Unnerved, she stopped writing for a while, but he continued to send letters, one containing a proposal without qualifiers. She began writing again, although she held off on a response, and when he left Japan for his graduate studies, she was there at the airport. Another year passed, and when he proposed a third time, she was ready with a yes.

"So I boarded a plane from Tokyo to Boston," my mother said, "with a *daikon* in my purse."

I nodded. The story of how she had flown halfway around the world carrying almost nothing but the *daikon*, the white Japanese radish my father had been longing for, was lore in our family, the sweetness of her gesture unsullied and maybe even enhanced by the years of acrimony, abuse, and infidelity that followed.

"We had a few good years in Boston and then a few more when we lived in Princeton," she said. "It was when we lived in Japan for those two years that he began to lose his mind." Late one night, Shoichi woke her to tell her to alert the authorities. He needed five hundred soldiers to protect their home: the enemy was coming, and they were prepared for attack. He was an alien, a prince who'd escaped from another world in a small computer. But the alien enemies had found him at last, and hiding was no longer an option.

Shoichi became angry when she refused to call the police. All night he kept talking about the enemy, jerking my mother awake every time she fell asleep. He stayed at home in this state for three days, until finally she did call the authorities: first his father and then the hospital.

This was in the early seventies; I was seven. I didn't think I could recall any of it when my mother first began speaking, but as she continued there was a flicker, a memory of my father standing on a table, backlit by the Tokyo sunset and yelling as my sisters and I scurried around on the ground and cried.

He was restrained, sedated, and borne away. As soon as my mother received permission from his doctors, she visited him at the hospital. He greeted her with a look of polite confusion. Then his face cleared. "Oh, I know you," he said. "You have three daughters, don't you."

To reassure herself more than him, she reached out to touch his hands. They were so cold that for a moment she wondered if he was in fact an alien.

They would stay together for seven more years. He'd take to wandering outside the Imperial Palace in Tokyo, saying that he had important secrets to impart to the emperor. She flew out to Italy to rescue him when, instead of delivering a paper on the levitated superconductor multipole experiment, he ranted to hundreds of stunned physicists from all over the world that he needed to see the pope because he was Christ reborn. He'd end up in the hospital again and again, and at his father's insistence my mother would explain to colleagues and friends that he was there for a heart condition, a lie that would become the truth more than three decades later. We'd return to Princeton because she, missing America, wore him down, something my father never forgave her for, and they would fight and have affairs. At his lab, colleagues and former students would shun him and dismiss his ideas, citing his megalomania and illness, and he'd drink too much, kick and punch us with increasing ferocity, and become a regular at the local mental institution, until one blustery day in April, when he was away on one of his long trips to Japan, we'd pack up and move away, leaving just a note behind.

But it was when he failed to recognize her for the first time that my mother realized that in order to survive, she would have to pull away from him.

"It was hard at first, and then—" Her voice, when she continued, was low. "Then it wasn't."

I knew she'd been struggling since the memorial service, wondering whether she should have stayed, if she could have saved him.

"You were right to pull away," I said. "If you hadn't left him, you wouldn't be around now, and who knows where we'd be. You know that, don't you?"

She brushed aside a phantom wisp of hair and looked down at her hands. In her mid-seventies she was still beautiful, the delicacy of her features undiminished by age. "I know."

I took a deep breath. "Just one last question," I said. "Do you think—" Somewhere along the way my eyes had filled. I slashed at them with an arm. "Did he ever love you?"

She glanced at me before looking away again. Then she said the phrase that I thought of as the refrain of my childhood. "He was sick."

"But that didn't mean he couldn't—"

"And he loved physics so much," she said. "There wasn't a lot of space left after that." Her eyes met mine. "So no. No, I don't think he ever did."

She spoke without rancor. It was a long time ago, and she knew as well as I did that if my father hadn't loved her back, it was his tragedy rather than hers.

I was lugging my suitcase down the stairs on the last day of my visit when my mother called to me from the second floor. I looked up. Her face was flushed, and she was waving a small black book. Back in Princeton, she said, Toshiko-san had given her Shoichi's address book so she could call relatives and friends who needed to be informed of his death. She'd been going through it and had just discovered a current address for Masako-san, the girl he'd liked in high school. "You know, the one that made him reluctant to marry me."

She'd seen her once, she said, at the airport on the day Shoichi departed for Boston. A host of his friends had gathered to see him off. Masako-san was the only other girl in the crowd, and my mother had known at once who she was.

She was small, smaller even than herself, my mother said, and delicate and poised. She had a Mona Lisa smile, and she smiled a lot at my father that day, though she'd cried, too.

She had lupus. Shoichi's parents had forbidden him to marry her because they feared that his children would inherit the condition. Other Japanese parents would have felt the same, which was why my mother knew that Masako-san could never have married.

My mother waved the address book again. "Don't you see, he kept in touch with her," she said. "He never forgot her."

I was still, imagining my father bent over a girl even smaller than my mother, a crowd of his friends pressing in on him as the time for his departure drew near. I thought of him writing to her, going to see her when he was in Tokyo, and missing her when he was away.

"Maybe he loved her all his life," my mother said.

She looked hopeful, even though what she was saying was that the relationship that had consumed twenty-four years of her life had been a sham from the start, and I knew that somehow she'd sensed what was behind all my questions.

"Maybe he always missed her," she said. "Maybe all the other women in his life somehow fell short."

I smiled. For a moment I'd been swept up by the story. But a high school crush that had lasted all his life—it was the stuff of movies. What she'd handed me was a Rosebud moment, and I was too earthbound to believe it could explain my father.

"I don't know about that," I said.

"You sure?" she asked, but the hopeful look was already fading. "Well, maybe you're right. It's hard to know anything about anyone, isn't it?"

"Especially him," I said.

She laughed. "That's true."

Looking up at her, I had a sudden urge to tell her everything. That I was guilt-stricken about not having returned my father's last phone call to me, three weeks before his death. How shocked I'd felt when my father's MIT friend said that Shoichi believed his disorder ruined his life: whether because I was naïve or optimistic or in denial, I hadn't realized that he considered—that he knew— his life was ruined. I wanted to confess how small I'd felt at the funeral home, when my own grief proved a pale, flimsy thing next to Toshiko-san's, and what I'd just understood, that behind my inquiry into my father's relationships lay my own guilt and fear. Because if my father had never loved the wives and girlfriends who loved him and nursed him and stayed by his side, what hope was there for me, the daughter who'd fled his home and returned as seldom as she could? If I relayed these thoughts to my mother, perhaps she could untangle them and smooth them back into something less terrible.

Yet nothing she could say would explain my father. Whether because of his devotion to physics, his illness, or a deficiency deep inside him, he'd never loved any of us, at least not in any way that mattered. Besides, she'd suffered enough because of him. There was no reason to add to the guilt she felt for all the ways his life weighed down my sisters' and mine. Far better to tell her the one definite conclusion I'd reached since his death: he linked me to her, and for that I would always be grateful.

But the airport taxi was crunching gravel outside, and with a sigh she was beginning to make her way down the stairs. For now we were out of time.

So I squinted up at her instead. "Masako-san, huh?"

She shrugged. "It's nice to think so, isn't it?"

And I told her that it was, and I wished with all my heart that I could.

UNBEATABLE

For decades I thought it was a dream, and perhaps it was. I wake to the sound of people arguing outside. They're grown-ups, men; some are speaking Japanese. I don't recognize their voices. At last I hear my father, his voice raised. He's talking so fast his words no longer sound like any language I know. When he's finished, there's silence.

I'm young enough that I have to stand on tiptoe to peer out the window. The edge of its frame digs into my forearms. The sun is just rising. There's my mother, standing between the dogwood and the birch in the yard, her face in shadow. My father is getting into his long white Impala, and on the driveway behind his car is a row of men holding hands. They seem to flutter, a paper people chain in the breeze.

A few months after his death, my mother told me the story. My father had been manic for days, roaming the house naked and muttering about the CIA and KGB tapping his phones. In the middle of the night, he rose from their bed and began packing. He had to go to the casinos. God had said so. He'd been chosen. He was blessed. *Unbeatable.* God had promised he would make millions.

My mother pleaded. He wasn't thinking straight. Princeton to Atlantic City was a two-hour drive, and my father was in no shape to make it. He hadn't eaten or slept for days. Didn't he remember that last accident? What if he had another one? Maybe they could take a trip to the hospital instead.

When my father ignored her, rummaging through her purse and different drawers in the house to pull together a bundle of cash, she phoned one of his colleagues at his lab. It wasn't long past four in the morning, but after speaking with her, the colleague, another physicist, must have made some calls himself. Within the hour he and three other physicists, one more colleague and two of my father's grad students, had arrived at our house.

When my father came to the door, they began to wheedle. They needed my father, they said. They needed him healthy and well rested, back at work. They were so close to their goal. How would they get there without him? They'd be happy to shuttle him to Atlantic City and throw some dice down with him—if *sensei* would just hand over the keys? They offered to get a blackjack game up and running in another hour right here in Princeton, right here in Shoichi-san's house.

My father barely seemed aware they were there. Wild-eyed, his face set, he pushed past them and ran to his car.

The physicists moved so quickly, my mother said, they must have planned it beforehand. Marshaling themselves on the driveway, they took each other's hands, a human barricade.

My father jerked the car into reverse. He didn't come at the physicists fast, but neither was he stopping. They were brave and loyal and they held their ground, with only a faint tremor to betray their fear, for a few seconds before they broke, releasing each other's hands and scattering as they dove for the lawn, and then my father was gunning it to Atlantic City.

WORK EQUALS FORCE
TIMES DISPLACEMENT

The memorial for my father was held in a Hyatt on the strip mall–lined highway that connects Princeton, that most idyllic of college towns, to the rest of the world. It was early December, a month after his death, and cold and bleak. Outside, a fitful rain fell. Inside, the air was musty, and despite stabs at elegance—a red carpet, oversized chandelier, a mirror for a wall—the gathering place looked like what it was, a cramped conference room. As a fusion energy researcher and physicist, my father had had an international reputation, and he'd worked at his lab for more than forty years. But he was imperious and known for being contemptuous of others, and when he died, he'd been retired a full decade. I was sure that most guests had shown up out of a sense of duty, as I had.

When I was young and my father was still capable of charm and even sweetness, I never wanted to be apart from him, but as he became more and more violent over the years, we grew apart. When I was fifteen and my mother finally gave in to my sisters' and my pleas to leave him, moving us out during one of his long trips to Japan, I felt nothing but relief. So in the weeks after his death, I was taken aback by the thickness of the fog I found myself in—indeed, by the fact I was in a fog at all.

By the morning of the memorial, I knew that the fog couldn't be grief. Pity and confusion, more like, along with guilt at how I'd cut him out of my life. In my mid-forties, I was close to my mother and stepfather, fulfilled by my work, and happy in my relationship. I wouldn't miss my father, I told myself, nor would I wish him back. Seven of my father's colleagues had asked to eulogize him, and eager to fill seats, my sisters and I had said yes to them all. At the service they stood one by one, aging men in crumpled suits, and spoke of Shoichi as their leader and guide. His brilliance—"That's a word," said another, "that I'm betting you'll hear more than once today"—was legendary. If at times he was a little arrogant, prone to making mincemeat out of those with less ability—well, he went on with a shrug, with a mind so dazzling, could you really blame him? According to another, they'd all shared in the hope of fusion, but it was my father's idealism, his passion and commitment, that spurred and galvanized them. One eulogist said he could never forget how Shoichi had turned down a job in the budding field of computers in the early sixties, even though he knew it was the wave of the future: he'd been that confident he could crack fusion and deemed it the more vital step for mankind.

Listening from my seat in the front row, my own eulogy clutched tightly in my hand, I took it all in under advisement. I knew few specifics about my father's work. He and I never spoke about fusion. I'd done poorly in high school algebra, which earned from him two blue knots along my jawline and a sand-dollar-sized bump on the head, and I grew up to be a novelist. What I did know was that my father had hungered for glory, the Nobel Prize the goal around which he built his life. His colleagues were just doing their duty as eulogists, making the departed look good through spin, hyperbole, or outright lies—and I, the last speaker, would do the same.

While composing my speech, I'd asked my mother for an anecdote that would convey Shoichi's commitment to physics. She told me, her laughter shaky, how he'd gotten out of bed to work on an equation during their wedding night. At his memorial I retold the story, concluding with my one line of sincere praise: "That's a man who loved his work." That the man's devotion to his wife fell short— that the anecdote hinted at the divorce that lay in their future—I left for the audience to infer.

Growing up, my father seemed destined for greatness. Even as an infant, he showed exceptional intelligence and curiosity. His father, a scientist, and his grandfather, a doctor, nurtured his interest and promise in science and math.

He received the highest marks in the country on the exam to enter the University of Tokyo. While there he won awards, acclaim, and, finally, a full fellowship to MIT. When he decided to take it, Japan's biggest newspapers ran articles deploring the "brain drain" that was stealing minds such as his to America. He completed his doctorate at MIT in just three years, with a dissertation on how plasmas, clouds of disassociated atoms, transport mass, energy, and momentum, and at twenty-seven he was hired to work on fusion at Princeton's Plasma Physics Laboratory, or PPL.

Fusion energy is modeled on the sun and the stars. In a chaotic dance, the nuclei of four hydrogen ions merge to form a single nucleus of helium. The new nucleus is lighter than the original four, and the difference in the mass is converted into energy. But using ordinary hydrogen, as the sun does, takes billions of years, so scientists have focused instead on combining two hydrogen isotopes, deuterium and tritium, which react together quickly.

My father worked on what were and still are fusion's two central obstacles: how to produce and sustain the high temperatures, more than a hundred million degrees Celsius, necessary for a reaction, and then how to safely contain that reaction. The PPL was founded on the belief that the key to these problems is plasma, which out of all the states of matter allows atomic particles to move the fastest, thus increasing the chances of fusion occurring. Per the obituary submitted by the lab, my father had been among the first in America to "appreciate the advantages of the tokamak concept." In the sixties, scientists and engineers constructed different fusion reactor machines all around the world, and in the Russian-designed tokamak, magnetic fields held the hot plasma inside a donut-shaped bottle, which accommodated the particles' movement while also containing it. Its results rapidly eclipsed those of other fusion research devices. My father also designed and led experiments to figure out why plasma had been lost in earlier models, and in the late sixties he invented a new kind of magnetic bottle, the Spherator, to hold fusion plasmas.

Solid contributions, if not the achievements his promise had presaged. Yet they came at a price. Overwhelmed by stress, he drank to excess. Working long hours, as on his wedding night, he wore himself out. Acutely aware in his twenties and thirties that physics is a young man's game, he spoke often about blowing his brains out before he turned forty. He resented and, at times, hated us, his family, for using up his time and energy. Every October for years, long after fusion had been widely deemed a bust, he was in a torment of anticipation and anxiety in the days leading up to the announcement for the Nobel. Weeks passed before his rage and despondency ebbed.

After the memorial, my mother, sisters, and I dispersed, my mother heading back to England and my sisters to California, where they work—one as a yoga teacher, the other as a manager in a Silicon Valley company—and raise children. I stayed on the East Coast with Rob, a filmmaker and fellow professor.

Through the winter the fog didn't lift. I was sleeping badly, neglecting and sometimes even snapping at Rob, and missing student appointments and writing deadlines. By the spring it was clear that for my health, marriage, and career, I needed to find a way out.

The problem, I thought, was doubt. For years I'd longed to be free of my father, and now I finally was. The fog that I was in had to be about the tributes that I heard at the memorial. Long ago I'd come to a conclusion about my father: cruel, bullying, and obsessed with winning glory for his work, he was unworthy of respect all around. Because of this assessment, I'd cut him out of my life, and felt good about doing so. If this appraisal wasn't correct—I didn't know what followed that *if,* and that seemed the most likely reason for how enveloping the fog was, how dense.

If I knew that his colleagues had been dissembling, if I were positive that my father had always and only been interested in fusion as the quickest path to the Nobel, the fog would surely clear. So I was surprised to find myself yearning to discover that the eulogies had contained some truth. I wanted to believe that at least a part of my father had been good: idealistic, high-minded, generous. In the end, it seemed, I'd rather be proud of him, even if that meant I'd have to live with the knowledge that I judged and treated him unfairly—even if that meant yet more guilt.

Although my mother hadn't seen or spoken to my father for more than twenty-five years when he died, no one knew him better as both prodigy and disappointment. In May I visited her and my stepfather in their manor house outside of Bath, and the morning after my arrival she took a break from her writing in order to take me around her garden. Her irises were in full bloom; before us the valley rolled out, a pastoral dream of sheep, paddocks, and trees. Though thinner than she should have been, my mother was in good spirits.

When I asked if my father had regretted working on fusion, she looked blank.

"People, including you, always say he loved it," I said. "But it never seemed as if he enjoyed it. Not the day-to-day of it, anyway."

"In the beginning, when he was young, he was passionate," she said. "But as time went on—" She hesitated. "I suppose he felt frustrated."

"I don't get that," I said. "You love writing itself, right? Some days it's outright torture, other times it's tedious, but when it's going well, when it's really flowing, there's nothing else like it."

A magpie rose from a tree. My mother's eyes tracked its movement across the sky. "What if you knew your work was never going to get published?" she asked. "If you knew no one would ever read you."

She had a point. Not getting read would drain my satisfaction. It'd be as if the writing hadn't happened. But the delight I took in doing the work, the deep pleasure of stitching words together and seeing a world emerge and take shape: wouldn't that remain? Or would enough bitterness, later, seep into and taint that memory, too?

"Is that what science is like?" I asked. "If something doesn't work, does it seem as if everything you've discovered and learned along the way didn't happen?"

"I don't know. For him, maybe."

"But fusion," I said. "It was so unlikely."

"That's why he picked it. It was the hardest problem he could find."

"And he was arrogant enough to think he could solve it."

My mother frowned. "Fusion was a great goal," she said. "It still is. If the lab had figured out fusion back in the seventies or even the eighties—" She swept out a hand, a gesture that took in the trees, her irises, the sky above.

"Think how different the world would be now." There was a throb to her voice. "Think how different the future would be."

"Yes, but Daddy didn't know about climate change back then," I said. "No one did."

Another frown. "At the memorial," she said, "someone said he thought about doing computers, but that wasn't accurate. His first and real passion was theoretical physics." His MIT advisors had encouraged him in this pursuit. Because it didn't involve as much collaboration as fusion, she said, they'd thought it a better fit.

"But your father—" She paused.

Stricken, suddenly certain that she was about to say that he thought fusion the surer route to the Nobel, I said, "My father what?"

"He believed in fusion," she said. "He thought it would happen, and sooner rather than later." She threw me a glance. "He was a good man, inside."

He's good inside: it was her go-to phrase. Did she actually believe it?

Maybe she didn't. That would make sense, given how my father used to beat her—how he'd even torn up her paintings in fits of jealousy over her success as an artist and writer. Maybe she could tell that I was hoping his life wasn't a waste, that he was worthy of respect, and was trying to convince me of what she knew was a falsehood, so I'd breathe easier. Maybe she wanted to convince herself—overcome by guilt and remorse, she might have suppressed how he terrorized and hurt her.

Or maybe she did believe he was good. She'd known him when he was at his most incandescent. Perhaps those memories blinded her still.

For decades I all but forgot about fusion. I wanted to sideline my father, of course. But the world had also moved on. Fusion was a pipedream. There was no one solution for the global energy problem, no saving the world in a single superhero swoop.

And when the new wind turbines, giant and white and spiky, began sprouting across the landscape and solar panels started taking over cornfields and suburban rooftops, I felt vindicated, if less triumphant than I'd thought.

It was Rob who set me straight. Five years ago, on our first date, I'd told him what my father did. His eyes had widened. Back in high school, he said, he'd argued about energy in a debate contest. It was the 1970s, and the exhaust in the air was choking, cars idling outside gas station for hours, and when he learned about fusion, he'd felt thrilled and just plain old *relieved*. The thought that we'd soon channel the power of the sun made him believe, made him *see*, that human ingenuity and optimism would always win out. *If we could do that, what couldn't we do?*

His excitement aside, I thought Rob's take on fusion generally aligned with mine. It was a beautiful dream, sure. If I'd understood, back then, what fusion could be and what it would have meant, it would have thrilled me, too. Hell, I'd still feel thrilled—if it had worked.

In the spring after my father's death, I asked Rob if he'd help me to research fusion. It'd mean digging into the archives, I said; there couldn't be much that was current. Rob replied that his bet was that there'd be a trove of contemporary material. Even if fusion wasn't front-page news, he said, the people who counted hadn't given up. A massive undertaking like that, arguably more complex than anything ever attempted, including space travel: it took time. There was the big lightbulb moment, the genesis of the concept, and then thousands of other smaller flashes that went into making the concept happen.

That part might be grueling and often tedious, Rob said, but it was just as crucial—and to him, just as thrilling and inspiring. *That's the work.*

As an energy source, fusion is the stuff of bad science fiction, too good to be believable. It doesn't involve drilling, mountaintop mining, or burning, which means no oil spills, pipelines, deforestation, wildlife endangerment, polluted waterways, acid rain, smog, or greenhouse gases. Unlike wind and solar, its output would be non-intermittent, available on tap, and enormous, more than enough to light up cities; power factories; cool Malaysian skyscrapers and heat Alaskan schools; propel cars, buses, trucks, and high-speed rail; and someday, if the technology could be worked out, fire up planes or blast rockets to the moon and distant planets. Unlike fission, which requires massive, lethally unstable processing plants, fusion wouldn't lead to a Chernobyl or Fukushima. Best of all is that its fuel, deuterium and tritium, can be extracted from seawater, a cheap and essentially inexhaustible source.

In 1961, when my father started working at PPL, interest in fusion was cresting. The research had begun in America in the 1950s, when innovations such as dishwashers were finding their way into homes, and it took off in the sixties, when the space program stoked America's imagination and its love affair with science and technology was at its peak. Through the seventies, the Arab oil embargo as well as belief in fusion's promise continued to fire media attention and funding, with articles appearing regularly in the major papers and journals.

As late as 1983, *Vogue* had a full-page photo of my father standing inside part of his lab's tokamak, alongside a breathless write-up: "A modest proposal: solve the world's energy crisis by developing a safe, clean, practical, commercially viable method of producing electricity. That's what scientists at Princeton University's Plasma

Physics Laboratory set out to do, and today—astonishingly—they're very, very close." In the photo the tokamak, a 1970s vintage version, resembles a giant tractor tire festooned with string. My father, standing inside what would be the rim, looks handsome and confident, his arms folded and his feet braced, the bloat of alcoholism not yet apparent in his face.

Only a year or two later the excitement was gone, drained by a string of well-publicized failures. By the mid-eighties, which is when I remember it best, my father's lab seemed quiet and a little sleepy, a place where smart men dutifully toiled. The funding was drying up and with it, perhaps inevitably, their optimism. They were beginning to suspect that if their lab did manage to make fusion a viable energy source, it wouldn't be in their lifetime.

In my research, I kept coming back to that. As a power source, fusion wasn't *viable*. It wasn't economically feasible, because the energy required to produce the conditions for the reaction was always more than the energy that was created. For practical intents and purposes, the scientists were still short of their goal. Yet they did succeed. They brought two hydrogen atoms together and generated energy, replicating the process of the sun on earth.

Back from England, I began corresponding with Sam, a lab colleague of my father's, and a week later I was meeting him in the lobby of the Princeton University cafeteria. I didn't know him—the widow of another physicist had put us in touch—and I was delighted to see that he'd brought along another colleague, T.K. A Chinese immigrant, T.K. was the father of a high school classmate and a family friend I remembered with fondness.

At the table, when I thanked Sam for meeting with me—I told him I really wanted to understand my father's relationship to his work—he nodded. He'd been like so many others when he began working at the lab in the early 1970s, he said: in awe of my father's brilliance. Only later did they become friends.

He was probably around sixty, a generation younger than my father, and he still taught and worked at the lab. I'd contacted other colleagues of my father whom I knew, men like T.K. who'd been friends with my mother. But perhaps because they'd known me since childhood, they were less forthcoming in our email exchanges, repeating the bromides of the memorial. *A great mind,* they'd say, and, in an echo of my mother: *A good man.*

Sam's emails, by contrast, were direct and incisive. To wit, his assessment of my father's career: *He had many brilliant ideas, some of which came to fruition in the construction of major and successful fusion-oriented devices. But assembling and motivating teams is part of the work here, and I don't recall your father being successful in that.*

A plate of stew in hand, T.K. took his seat. I remembered him as a merry soul, always beaming. When I asked if he was still working, he laughed and said he'd retired almost twenty years ago. "But I still go to the lab every day," he said. "They can't get rid of me so easily."

I asked when he'd started.

He was in grad school, he said, finishing his degree, with a job offer on the table for $1,200 a month, when he'd received a telegram from the PPL director. "The director was *the* word in plasma physics," he said, "but he was only offering $900, and I was newly married. I thought I'd do it just a year."

"And then what happened?" I asked.

T.K. laughed again. His laugh was outsized, and so infectious I had to smile. "Once you do fusion," he said, "you don't care about anything else."

Sam inclined his head. "It's easy to be in love with it."

Reaching for my notepad, I asked why that was.

"There's the utility to the world," Sam said. "That's one. Second is the beauty of physics. Third, fusion is a really, really complex problem. Look, it's already avoided being solved for half a century or more."

"According to my mother," I said, "the third reason is why my dad loved it."

Looking serious, they both nodded.

"And you think fusion will be solved?" I asked.

"I do," Sam said.

He spoke with such conviction that in that moment I, too, felt sure.

"Of course," he added, "the research has to go in the right direction. Right now, because of what's happening in France—" He checked to see if I was following.

I'd read about the project. Known as ITER, located in France and financed and run by a consortium of countries including Japan and the US, an attempt to build the world's largest and most powerful tokamak. "You don't agree with what they're doing?"

An emphatic headshake. "And because of that program, other programs are being sucked dry," he said. "In the sixties, things were different. Back then, you blew your nose and got funding."

"Because people believed in fusion," I asked, "or because science funding was better?"

"Both," Sam said. "The scientists won the war."

The answer wasn't what I'd expected.

"But it was fusion, too," he continued. "People had confidence it would happen."

T.K. said the work they'd done at the lab had been different back then. I asked him to explain, and he said that when he and my father started, there weren't computers they could use. Together he and Sam described what they did instead, not just solving equations on paper but something to do with coating a Polaroid photo with some substance and waiting for the results to appear, which often entailed staying in the lab until late at night. I wasn't clear on the process, its point, or its appeal, but T.K. and Sam were animated, aglow with nostalgia, interrupting each other to make me understand.

All around us in the cafeteria, students laughed and chatted in pairs or groups. Though so much older, in their optimism and engagement with life and learning, T.K. and Sam fit right in.

Sam said that he and T.K. had had a bet. They'd never gotten the plasma to more than a million degrees, and T.K. thought they never would.

"But then we got to three million," Sam said, "and now we're up to five, and T.K. owes me a bottle of very fine wine."

They laughed.

Even more than the anecdotes they were telling, their easy camaraderie put me in mind of movies like *Apollo 13*, narratives in which sharp thinkers, usually but not always men, come together, armed with nothing but smarts, determination, and can-do spirit, and triumph over great obstacles to create, innovate, and launch into the cosmos. The brotherhood of scientists: it's a genre that Rob, starry-eyed about collaboration and enthralled by science and space travel, loves, and no wonder. They're romantic tales, brimming over with hope and uplift.

My father's storyline had been different.

As Sam and T.K. continued to reminisce, I became aware of a refrain. *It was a different era.* They didn't sound wistful—they were too practical and grounded for that—but the phrase sounded a lower, more melancholy note.

As the joke, by now an old chestnut, went, *Fusion is the energy of the future—always just twenty years away.* In science-team movies, the most exhilarating part usually comes at the three-quarters point, when the goal heaves into view, just out of arm's reach. If that moment were stretched out over decades, where would all the adrenalin, that pent-up excitement, go? For some, it might curdle into resentment and rage.

But maybe that wasn't right. That picture my father had painted of himself at the lab, a giant surrounded by intellectual mice who sometimes helped but were more often underfoot, tripping him up: maybe he didn't always see himself that way. Maybe he'd known the fizzy joy of collaboration, of working shoulder to shoulder with a mate or team.

"If I could ask," I said.

Sam and T.K. turned as one.

"I know my father went to parties," I said. "But did he partake in the work culture—did he exchange ideas, make bets, enjoy working with you all?"

They exchanged a glance. "Your father—" Sam began, and then stopped. "He was so brilliant," he said, as T.K. nodded.

Home again after meeting with Sam and T.K., I continued to read about fusion, but I was just going through the motions. There was no hope. My initial assessment had been correct. My father, at work, was the man I'd known: neither high-minded nor generous.

On a hot July afternoon, I was sprawled on the floor with our new kittens, when all at once I recalled one of Sam's lines. *The scientists won the war.*

The scientists had split the atom and created the nuclear bomb.

My father had been nine when the bomb destroyed Hiroshima and Nagasaki. In the days that followed, he would have seen the photos of the devastated cities and heard about the hundreds of thousands who'd been burned, injured by falling debris, and poisoned by radiation. He learned about the flash, bright enough to blind and filled with so much radioactivity it vaporized human beings, leaving only a shadowy imprint in their place; the pressure wave that followed, collapsing entire buildings; the blast of heat that left everything in its wake in flames; the second pressure wave which, moving in the other direction, swept away anything still left standing; the mushroom cloud that bloomed over the scenes of apocalypse; and, finally, the black rain of radioactive particles.

By all accounts, my father had been a sensitive, highly intelligent boy, and nine was an impressionable age. How did he find out that the humble atom was responsible for the bombs' almost supernatural force—the radio, a schoolyard rumor, or a teacher who recognized his precocity? No, most likely it was his father who took him aside and explained. As a scientist, he was probably clear and direct, and Shoichi, who would be celebrated in later years for his powers of concentration, would have listened intently, not missing a word.

Afterward, as Shoichi studied the newspaper photos of concrete rubble, twisted and melted steel girders, and miles of razed wooden homes, maybe he wondered at the might of the atom. Maybe he dreamed about mastering and harnessing the force of the atom for peaceful and productive ends. Maybe those hopes shaped a career.

I emailed Sam. *Could my father's experiences during the war have inspired his research into fusion energy?* I asked, citing Hiroshima and Nagasaki. *Or is that farfetched?*

Sam wrote back the next morning. *It's an interesting possibility,* he said. *The earliest conferences on fusion were called "Peaceful Uses of the Atom."*

I grew up listening to my mother's recollections of the war. The bombs that leveled buildings in her hometown of Nagoya; the makeshift shelter that she and her family hid in every night, a hole in the ground that her father and brothers had dug and covered with wooden boards and clumps of earth; the death of her classmate, Misa, in an explosion. Soon after the bombing began, my mother was sent to the countryside, away from the frontlines, along with her mother and two of her siblings. Food was scarce. In one story, her ten-year-old sister swings upside down on the monkey bars, her hair falling forward, and my mother sees a sizable bald spot on the side of her head. Yet they managed, catching and cooking the insects that fed on rice plants—*they eat so much rice,* my grandmother had explained, *they're practically the same thing*—and searching the mountains for *akaza,* an edible weed, and in my mother's stories those years were a time of freedom.

My father never talked about the war. Even my mother only knew what he'd been through in bullet points: That Japan attacked Pearl Harbor when Shoichi was six, a little more than a year after his mother had died of pneumonia. That Shoichi's father decided to keep him in Tokyo, where bombing was constant. That he was so malnourished his stomach swelled.

The war had clearly informed my mother's career. The book she was working on involved trips to Japan as well as extensive research and long and numerous interviews with veterans. Before that was a collection of essays about British POWs who had been incarcerated and tortured by Japanese soldiers, and before that a novel, her first book in English, that traced the fortunes of a Japanese family from the late 1800s to the postwar period.

Was it possible that the war had played a part in my father's career, too?

And if it had—if my father elected to work on fusion because he wanted to transform the war's horrors into something that would help save the world—then maybe my mother wasn't completely wrong. Maybe there was good inside him.

I reread Sam's email one last time. It was the middle of the morning, not yet teatime in England. I reached for the phone.

As I explained, the words tumbling out, all I'd recently learned, my mother was quiet. Turning the revelation over in her mind, I assumed, but when I finished and she began speaking, her voice was measured, with just a hint of surprise.

"I thought you knew," she said. "I thought you'd figured out that connection." Of course the war had influenced his career choice. "After all, Hiroshima and Nagasaki had an impact on everyone in Japan."

It was my turn to be silent.

These days, she continued, she often found herself thinking about the bomb—something to do with her age, maybe, or the fact that she was the only Japanese person for miles around. Or maybe it was just her current project.

"Even if your father didn't think about the war every day," she said, "some days he must have."

She'd been writing when I called. I pictured her, tiny and fragile, sitting in her study with its spectacular views of the garden, her head tilted toward the phone and her feet propped up on her desk, papers and books in neat piles around her.

"But your father," my mother continued, "I wouldn't call him an idealist. He wasn't working to save the world."

The wire hummed. "His motivations were pure, just not in the way you're thinking." He'd worked on fusion, she said, because it was the question that intrigued him the most—and small wonder, imagine trying to solve the secrets of the sun!—and one he thought he could solve. "That's why he worked on it. Nothing more, nothing less."

I looked out the window, at the neighbors' roofs and treetops.

"What your father wanted above all," my mother said, "was to unravel the mysteries of the universe. What he wanted was to find truth."

She sounded solemn, and I understood that for her, as perhaps for me, the desire to know was no less noble than a quest to save the world.

Outside, trees rustled in the breeze.

My father had wanted to make the world a better place: by creating an alternative energy source, but more crucially by solving one of the mysteries of the universe and adding to the store of human knowledge. That he'd done so for his own reasons—because truth was beauty and bliss to him—didn't detract from the fact that he was an idealist, albeit of a very specific kind.

So yes, I could be proud of my father and his work—in fact I was proud. But that wasn't what I really wanted. Without realizing it, what I'd sought to know all along was how *he* felt about his work. Did he feel proud? Was his work worth it for him?

I thought of his rants about his unrecognized genius. Yet those started only when he was in his thirties, and achievement, or even a sense of accomplishment and satisfaction, wasn't the only way to measure worth.

My eyes pricked, the view in front of me blurring.

My father had loved his work. Not just what it stood for or what it could arrive at, but the actual work itself. This love hadn't endured; eventually it had been eaten away by time as well as resentment, jealousy, and spite. But when he was young, at least, in command of his powers and filled with hope, he found joy in it, and deep satisfaction. I felt that in my bones. He'd known then that truth might be beauty and bliss, but so was the search for it. So was the journey.

SNAPSHOT

I'd summoned them, and they had come.

My father had come home in a mood, or had had enough of my backtalk and was on a rampage. At some point I managed to pick myself off the floor and make a break for it. He tried to catch me by my hair and almost succeeded, but I was thirteen and could just about outrun him. I sprinted to his and my mother's bedroom and locked the door. There I ran to the heavy black phone on his side of the bed and, with shaking hands—he was banging and kicking on the door, shouting at me in English and Japanese to let him in or else, and the door was thin, how long could it hold—I managed to spin the dial around from nine and then one and one again. A woman answered and I said, sobbing and shuddering, that my dad was going to kill me and could she please send help and fast.

The *wee-ooh wee-ooh* of sirens sliced through the suburban quiet, sooner than I would have thought possible. The buzz of the doorbell, a few moments of silence followed by another buzz, and then—now my ear was pressed to the door—a volley of what sounded like frantic whispers. Next, a scurry of footsteps, the creak of the front door, the murmur of conversation, and then my mother, her voice cheery with just the slightest of tremors, her accent almost masked, was calling out to me: I could come out, it was safe, the policemen wanted to make sure I was okay.

They were here.

I unlocked the door, crept to the foyer, and felt startled.

I had an image of American cops. Tall and broad-chested, with deep voices and eyes that were hidden but watchful behind aviator shades: men, or more precisely, Starskys and Hutches. Streetwise types with a natural air of command, their bodies coiled for action, their hands resting ever so lightly on the guns at their hips. But these cops—were they really cops? They were babies. Indistinguishable from my sister's high school classmates: White boys with soft unformed faces and round eyes. We lived in Princeton, New Jersey, sheltered and elite, so maybe I shouldn't have been surprised. They wore uniforms, though, and weighing down their holsters—yes, those were guns. Yet the cops greeted me without meeting my gaze. As if it was their first assignment, and maybe it was, they huddled close together. They blushed, unable to hide their discomfort, their sheer embarrassment at being there.

They couldn't help me. After summoning them to our house— after tattling on my father—I was on my own.

While he stood by, the baby cops asked me what had happened. At first I couldn't speak, but then the words came, slowly. The cops took notes, looking sympathetic, and I thought I'd made a snap judgment. They were listening. They cared. They wanted to help, and knew how.

At last I was finished. The cops thanked me and put away their notepads. Then, turning to my father, they made him promise not to hurt me again. Once again I couldn't speak. Was that really all they were asking, a *promise,* mere words? Couldn't they guess how he'd punish me as soon as they were gone? But there was my father shuffling his feet. "Yes, of course," he was saying, "I understand," and my mother was nodding, her back straight and her face serious but calm; no one could have guessed that just half an hour before she'd been lying on the floor alongside me. The cops were nodding back, a nod fest all around; the relief in the room was obvious, and then they were all saying goodbye, the cops throwing more nods, but quicker ones, my way, and my mother was thanking them and then the door had shut and soon the cop car had pulled away.

Afterward, my father disappeared into the master bedroom. He kept to his promise for almost a week and then he was at it again, but the beatings weren't any worse than they had been, and he never mentioned the cops.

I don't know what power the policemen held over my father. Was it their guns, the authority of badges and uniforms, the color of their skin, or the furies they could unleash—handcuffs, jail, court, fines, public shame, deportation, professional and personal ruin?

Who can say.

But what I puzzle over more, now, are the cops.

At the time, I didn't just write them off as no help. I gave them a pass. *Baby cops.* Rookies, out of their depth. Later, I'd take the context into account. The late 1970s, a time when domestic abuse was rarely discussed. Probably the cops hadn't understood the fear and danger.

Now, though, I wonder if I wasn't the only one with Starsky and Hutch dreams. Maybe the cops wanted to be heroes. Maybe they'd joined the force to chase cars, foil bank robbers, and bust up drug cartels, to crack wise while staring down the barrel of a gun. *To protect and to serve.* To fight the good fight and keep the country safe.

A domestic squabble was small potatoes. Grunt work. A steppingstone to their real career.

Or was it something else?

When the door swung open, the cops saw a tiny Asian woman. Behind her a man, also Asian, in a shirt he was still buttoning up over his boxer shorts, his head bobbing or was he bowing, his accent so thick he could barely make himself understood. The girl didn't come out for a while. At first she didn't respond to their questions, her face hidden behind her hair, in shock, maybe, or just dumb or ashamed or shy, and the cops couldn't tell if she knew English. But she did. She got her story out. It just took a while because of her blubbering.

Did the cops also make a snap judgment? Did they see me as a foreigner, someone outside their care, whom they didn't need to protect? Maybe they saw my father as their favorite Chinese joint's waiter, servile and meek, no one who'd cause trouble. Maybe to them he was just another unthreatening math nerd, the Jap kid they'd bullied in the schoolyard.

Yes, that must be why they didn't take this 911 call seriously, this girl saying her dad was going to kill her.

AMERICAN FAIRYTALE

When my mother first came to America, she wore a pink coat with a rounded collar and four beveled black buttons. A farewell present from her parents and by far the most expensive garment she'd ever owned, the coat was wool, custom-made, and heavy enough to withstand the winters of Boston. It was March 1959. She was twenty-two and had never been outside of Japan or on a plane, and she'd not seen her fiancé, Shoichi, for a year, but she wasn't nervous, at least not much, or at least less nervous than excited. In her carry-on was a pocket Japanese-English dictionary, a copy of *A Little Princess*—later, she would name her second daughter after the heroine's doll, *Mako Emily*—and the daikon that she planned to grate, douse with soy sauce, and share with Shoichi for their first meal together in America.

Stepping out into Logan Airport felt unreal. Why were there so many people? No one had told her Americans' faces were more red than white, or that they liked to wear so much green. Even aside from the shape of her eyes, she stood out in her pink coat, and some glanced her way and frowned. But most were smiling and laughing; a few greeted her, offering a beer.

That Americans weren't always so friendly—that she'd arrived on a day called St. Patrick's—she learned soon enough. But in her telling, that arrival as well as the eighteen months that followed were a wonder.

My father was good to her, that was a lot of it. The bipolar disorder that would come to plague him hadn't manifested yet, and in the MIT physics department, where he was a grad student, he was already acclaimed as a star. But according to my mother, they were also lucky. The McCarran-Walter Immigration and Nationality Act, passed in 1952, meant that they and a few other select Japanese could now live and work in America. And as my mother told it, eighteen years after Pearl Harbor, the hatred that many Americans had felt for the Japanese was on the wane. Everyone was welcoming, everyone was kind.

At first she stayed in the house of my father's PhD advisor, a sweet man who called Shoichi the best mind at MIT. He and his wife made her feel at home. A week later, when my mother and father married, the advisor walked her down the aisle.

Boston had been colorless, the tree branches bare, when my mother first arrived. But in a few weeks a flower she'd never seen in Japan, forsythia, began to bloom. In the coming years she'd recreate it again and again in her paintings, her favorite harbinger of spring. My father's apartment, a drafty set of rooms with ceilings so high that my mother felt exposed, was a block from Symphony Hall. During the days and evenings, while my father was in class or the lab, she wandered their neighborhood. The sidewalks were red brick, the street lamps iron and ornate, their light soft. When she discovered one afternoon that the names of a set of streets nearby had a pattern—*Arlington, Berkeley, Clarendon, Dartmouth*—she was ecstatic, and wished she were brave enough to tap on the shoulders of passersby and let them know, in case they hadn't noticed.

In the fall, she began a Harvard master's program in literature, and she and my father moved across the river to a flat with an address that even now, six decades later, still makes her smile: *Harvard Street, Cambridge, Massachusetts.* The paint flaked; the wide-planked pine floors tipped so sharply she felt vertigo. In the mornings my father headed east to MIT while she went west to her classes, and in the evenings they regrouped for supper and home-work. My father was a favorite among the department secretaries; he and my mother were always being invited to dinner with his pro-fessors and their wives. They became friends with a Japanese man, an MIT engineering student, whose roommate had recently died. He visited them so often they joked they should have an extra bed-room for him.

The eloquence and learning of her professors and fellow stu-dents awed and humbled my mother. Was this the world she would have encountered had she been allowed to attend the University of Tokyo—an institution that loomed above all others in Japan, as if the Ivies, Stanford, and MIT were rolled into one—instead of the women's college, really no more than a finishing school, she'd gone to? Her English was poor, and she had to struggle to keep up with the reading. In a creative writing class, she wrote a poem about her life in Cambridge: frying up chrysanthemum leaves as tempura in her small kitchen, missing autumn in Tokyo despite the glory of the New England leaves, thinking she never wanted to leave America but feeling a homesickness for her country and language that was almost a physical ache. She's not a crier—I remember her weeping each of the three times that my father tore up her paintings, but only rarely when he beat her—yet when her professor praised and read out her poem to the class, she grew teary with gratitude and pride.

I was in college, the turbulence of my parents' break-up and its aftermath finally more or less behind me, when I began scratching at the fairytale. It peeled off in strips.

When she stayed at my father's advisor's home, she was jet-lagged and eager to see my father and explore her new city. But the advisor's wife had recently given birth to triplets, and my mother was asked to babysit.

In my father's last year at MIT, a professorship opened up in the physics department. My father, the odds-on favorite, was voted down by this same advisor, who persuaded his colleagues to choose another student.

My mother was a small Japanese woman who knew hardly any English. Though not unkind, the students in her Harvard classes rarely spoke to her, and never invited her out.

Although the McCarran-Walter Act allowed Asians to live in America, it had a quota of just two thousand per year. The roommate of my parents' friend, the engineering student, had also been Japanese. He'd been so lonely in Boston that one sunny afternoon he'd stepped in front of an oncoming train.

Growing up, I heard my father's rants against Americans—they hated us; they mocked his accent and laughed at him behind his back—only to dismiss them. In part this was because so much crazy talk—jealous of his brilliance, they were tapping his phones!—was strewn among his ravings: he was talking nonsense again; he was sick. But mostly I just couldn't believe in America's racism. My two sisters and I had been born in Princeton, where our parents had relocated after Boston, and they moved us "back" to Japan when I was seven, ostensibly for good. My first day of school in Tokyo, I walked into second grade and felt at once startled, unnerved, and gratified by how much the other children looked like my sisters and me. Yet at recess, those same kids formed a circle around me, so tight I gasped for air. They pulled my hair, shouted that I was a *gaijin,* and made fun of the way I spoke, dressed, and walked. Over time I learned the language and made friends, and eventually the bullying stopped, but I never felt Japanese. When my mother put her small foot down—*Japan is no place to raise daughters*—and we returned to Princeton after two years, my father was furious; their marriage never recovered. But my relief was profound. Japan had shown me that America was the only home I had.

For almost as long as I'd known my father, he'd been twisted with acrimony and grievance, and in the months that followed his death, when my guilt and regret over our long years of estrangement threatened to pull me under, I began sifting through his life for the source of his unhappiness. Only then did I recall his rants against racism and think, *of course.*

The light bulb should have blinked on earlier, that's clear. There was the way the other kids in Princeton had drawn back the skin at the corners of their eyes as I passed. There were the slurs, *Chink-Japslanteyesyellowface*, in the schoolyard and, later, on the streets of New York City, as well as the oh-so-well-meaning questions, aren't I a credit to the race and how did I learn to speak English so well and the hoariest of chestnuts, an oldie but still a goodie, *No no where did you* really *come from?*; there were the French lit *professeur* in college who said that she was pleased that I had some creativity, unlike the other Asian students who were *comme les robots*, and the classmate in grad school who told me that I wouldn't have trouble finding a professorship, not when I had the *diversity thing* going.

Whatever I experienced and still endure, my father had it worse. His tongue couldn't form certain sounds—why was his accent grating, when my mother's charmed?—and his ear couldn't distinguish them. He knew he spoke badly only from the bewilderment, incomprehension, and snickers of people around him.

He'd arrived in America in the late 1950s, less than fifteen years after World War II and the rounding up of Japanese Americans into camps. He would have regularly met veterans who'd been taught to hate and fear the Japanese; anti-miscegenation laws banning the marriage of Asians and White people were still in place. Ahead lay Vietnam; the rise of Japan as a world superpower and the inevitable backlash; the Japanese domination of the American auto market in the 1980s and the backlash to *that*, including the murder of Vincent

Chin, the young Chinese American man whom two Detroit men targeted, chased, and beat to death with a baseball bat because they thought he was Japanese and blamed him for the fact that they were out of work.

But how much had racism affected my father's career? He wasn't a migrant worker, grudgingly tolerated and regularly stiffed, but a privileged student with a plum fellowship to a prestigious university, and then a respected scientist and professor. Asians in math and science, in academia overall: heck, the stereotype might even have worked in his favor.

And he lived in Cambridge and then Princeton, liberal, intellectual enclaves filled with smart, successful immigrants.

So why did he hate living here? How much racism could he have faced?

The story I told myself for years was that my father's desire to return to Japan wasn't about America. It was because he wanted to live in a country where he was revered, his every word awaited and hung on. He wasn't being mistreated in America so much as he was missing the deference he was accorded as a professor and, even more importantly, as a man in Japan. Fixated on his own comfort, he willfully ignored the kind of life that my mother, sisters, and I would have had there—the limited opportunities, the brick load of expectations around husbands, children, and housework. In this narrative, he was the selfish patriarch and my mother, sisters, and I were the victims, and because of it, I never gave serious thought to what he lost and endured for our sake.

Still, even now, I can't quite let the story go. Because after my mother, sisters, and I decamped from his house—even after he retired from the university, when he had no reason, financial, personal, or legal, not to head for the hills—our father stayed in America. Why not leave, if it was so awful? Maybe the racism he'd experienced hadn't been that bad.

And yet. In high school I'd witnessed strangers and even my

classmates mocking him, pretending not to understand his accent for the pleasure of seeing how, in his frustration, he'd talk louder and faster, his face reddening and eyes bulging, spittle flying from his mouth, and how, afterward, his old habit would resurrect itself and he'd bow, his head jerking down and up as if yanked by string, despite his best efforts to control himself. While I, standing beside him, would flush, too, his shame and humiliation somehow my own, and long to sidle away. *No, I don't know that man.*

A warm and hazy day in late August, ten months after my father's death: I'm at home alone in the house Rob and I bought in Cambridge, two miles due west of the apartment that my parents had rented in 1960, and even though I should be working on the syllabi for the writing and lit courses that I'll be teaching in the fall, my mind keeps drifting. Finally giving up, I dial my mother's number.

As soon as she answers, I get right down to it, forget the chitchat.

Was the man who got the professorship at MIT instead of my father—too late, I realize that I'm assuming that it's a man, but could it really be otherwise—White? Was he American?

My mother says yes. He was a neighbor of theirs. She remembers him well. A bearish man, slow, large, and very gentle.

I ask how large a role racism had played in the decision.

After pausing to think, my mother says that more probably it was a question of personality. The man who got the job was docile, the opposite of my father. No, she doesn't think that my father's arrogance had put off the advisor. They remained friends for years.

When she says that Princeton, with its lab devoted to fusion research, was a better place for my father besides, my tone sharpens. If she's implying that Daddy had anything to do with the choice, I say, I'm not buying it. Doesn't she remember how sore he'd been about being passed over for the job, how he was still harping on it decades afterward? I say that that rejection was ground zero, the beginning of his downfall. In his view, it proved that the world was rigged against him and it presaged, perhaps even ushered in, the other disappointments, the missed honors and awards, that marked his career.

"Not getting that job changed him," I say, my voice flat.

My mother ponders this. Then she says that the advisor was smart, but not on the same level as my father. He might have felt jealous of him. "Or maybe your father alienated him," she says. "I thought he was a sweeter person back then, less arrogant. But maybe that's what happened."

I tell her that I want to explore how racism affected his career. "Even if it didn't influence his advisor's decision about the professorship, it must have changed Daddy's career trajectory in other ways."

My mother asks how I intend to research this.

"I'll poll his colleagues," I say.

"Even if there was racism," she says, "it's hard to prove."

There it is. The elusive, insidious nature of racism: How could my father know why he was passed over for promotions and awards? How could anyone?

"And then what?" she asks.

"What do you mean?" I say.

"If you find out he faced racism, what will you do?"

Wallow? Feel like shit? "I've learned a lot about him since he died," I say at last. "What will I do with any of it?"

At a loss, perhaps, she doesn't answer.

When I send out emails to my father's colleagues—*Do you think there was any truth to his claim that the lab and the university were racist?*—all their responses line up.

From one Japanese colleague: *No place is perfect since most people have some degree of racial prejudice, but the lab and the university are the least racially prejudiced places I know.* And from another: *In university politics, we foreign born might have some political disadvantages, but racism was not prevalent in the lab. Outside physicists complained that if they had foreign accents, they might be treated better.* According to the widow of one of my father's other colleagues: *I knew of no racism at the lab.* After listing several Japanese scientists who'd thrived at the lab, she writes, *Your father was not good at the "politics" of being a member of a group. This was undoubtedly exaggerated by his illness.*

Discouraged but still determined, I try Toshiko-san next. If anyone could tell me about the racism my father had encountered over the course of his life, it's she, a fellow native Japanese and his companion during his last decade. But when I phone her, I can't get a word in. She misses my father; another of her friends has died—*Soon no one left*—of course she sees her family, but most days she's at home by herself. At this point she still has my father's ashes, but soon they'll be buried in the cemetery and then *dōshiyo*. I listen, try to soothe, and eventually, feeling put out even as I'm weighing the benefit to myself—isn't she bound to say more in person?—I haul out my calendar and flip through it for a day I can drive to Princeton for lunch.

We meet in her place of choice, the restaurant in the Hyatt where my father's memorial was held, ten minutes away from her home in Trenton: tables in an atrium with shrubs in tubs and koi in an indoor pond, a buffet of indifferent meats and fish.

Despite what she said on the phone, Toshiko-san seems in good spirits, cheerful and lively as ever.

We eat and chat for almost an hour before I bore in. "My father probably talked to you about racism at work—"

She's shaking her head. "No."

Did he finally stop obsessing about racism? He was retired when he met Toshiko-san—had he moved on? Maybe he'd finally conceded that America wasn't so bad. Or had he found a new target for his rage?

"He never talk about work," she says.

"Never?" I say. "Really? I thought—" I break off. Her relationship with my father is a mystery. The more I've gotten to know and care about her, the more it confounds me.

I just hope he didn't put her down.

"You were so good to him," I say.

"He nice to me," she says, nodding, perhaps to herself. "He nice to me, too."

As she digs into her chocolate ice cream (my raspberry tart, sludgy and sour, congealing in a lump), I study her. She and I are the only Asians in the restaurant, and I had assumed that people would take us for mother and daughter, but—is it our looks, my simple shirt and jeans versus her staid blazer and slacks, or a formality between us?—while asking me about table preferences, the hostess referred to her as *your friend,* and against all expectations and logic, I'd felt disappointed.

When my father was alive, I felt grateful to Toshiko-san because her presence in his life meant that mine wasn't required, and because when we went out for our sushi dinners, her nonstop, almost stream-of-consciousness chatter took the onus of conversation off me. When did my feelings for her tip into something more? As a bow-tied blond boy runs past us and Toshiko-san swallows the last bit of her ice cream, the conviction grows in me that she and I *are* family, never mind what some know-it-all hostess thinks.

"When did you come to America?" I say. "Was it 1946?"

Toshiko-san says that she and her husband, the American soldier, had to wait for her papers to clear, so a little later than that. "'48," she says. Then, wrinkling her brow: "Or '49 *ka na.*"

"You didn't have much English—"

"A little." She pronounces it *rittle*. All the schools in Japan taught English, she says, but because of the war, she had only a year of high school.

I ask if her husband spoke Japanese; hadn't he been there for some time—

Laughing, she says that even after being stationed for five years in Kyoto, all he could manage was *konnichiwa*.

"You must have missed Japan," I say, "not to mention speaking Japanese."

Toshiko-san's shaking her head again. Her husband's family in Alabama was as sprawling as hers in Kyoto, and warm and kind. No, she and her husband never lived down there—they were in army bases in Indiana and then France for years before settling in Trenton. But they often visited his parents and siblings.

I tell her about what I read about Japanese war brides, how isolated they felt in America. There couldn't have been many other Japanese around?

She explains that in the army bases, there were many other Japanese wives. Nine, she says, maybe ten, a whole group of them. "All of us friends," she says.

When Toshiko-san smiles—she often does—her eyes look like a child's drawing of hills.

"You've really enjoyed your life, haven't you," I say.

Toshiko-san's smile widens. "Yes," she says, and again: "*Yes.*"

I ask what kinds of jobs she's had.

She says that in 1961, soon after she and her husband moved to Trenton and their brood already numbered four or five, she decided she wanted to go back to work. Her husband, she says, didn't want her to—*The house full of kids!*—but she was determined.

"Why?"

"It was summer," she says, scrunching up her face and fanning at it with her hand, "and the factory was *air-conditioned*."

She laughs with me.

When I prod, she says that she worked at two factories. The first manufactured parachutes for the government, but after a year, the work dried up. The second made electrical products, and she stayed for twenty-seven years, operating the power machines.

Was the job hard to get?

She says that she asked around first, to make sure that the factories hired Japanese. Work was scarce in those days, and when she showed up at the hiring office, fifteen people were waiting to apply for the same job. I interrupt, and she says yes, all of them born in America, men and women both. But she was the one they hired.

She thumps on her chest. "Japanese, *ne.*" *Japaneezu.*

"What does that have to do with it?" I ask. She's smiling so I am, too, but I'm thinking this is what I've been seeking, a tale of Japanese exploitation.

Her look says I shouldn't have to ask. "Japanese are best workers, everyone know that."

The next day, after reporting on my findings, I asked my mother if she was sure my father never mentioned a specific case of racism. "There must be something."

"I don't think he did," she says. "And I never found Americans that racist. Other than the writing on our street that one Halloween, I never—"

"Wait," I say. "What are you talking about?"

"Don't you remember?" The words had been terrible and hateful, she says, the letters enormous and in bright colors. Even though there'd been other Asian families on the block, the writing had only been in front of our house.

At first she says she doesn't remember what the words were. But by making guesses that she confirms or rejects, eventually I worm them out of her. There were the old standbys, *Go home* and *Jap-Chinkgook*, and words I didn't know she knew, *pussy* and *prick*. And obscene stick figures.

"Neighborhood kids, I guess," my mother says.

Someone I played Frisbee with, teenagers I'd passed trick-or-treating?

"They used some kind of special chalk," my mother says. She sounds a little tired, maybe, but otherwise fine. "I spent the entire day trying to get it out."

I search my memory for shameful words and drawings on pavement; my mother lugging a bucket, soapy water sloshing; on her hands and knees on the pavement scrubbing, and rising and dusting herself off when neighbors passed by in their cars.

"Are you sure I was there?" I ask.

"Oh yes."

Despite the world-class scientists and mathematicians populating our neighborhood, the street I grew up on was essentially 1970s-era suburbia. Houses, either colonial or modern, that sat on a quarter to half acre of lawn, trees, and flowerbeds. But even though all our nearest neighbors were White, many were European immigrants and a number were Jewish. The larger neighborhood included two Chinese American families. Our family didn't stand out, at least not much.

We borrowed sugar and eggs from our neighbors, and they from us. I played capture the flag with the kids on the block. On Easter we held egg hunts; in July we had sparklers; in November we ate turkey; in December we hung trinkets on a tree. Our house had some Japanese artifacts and features indoors—shoji screens to separate the foyer and the living room, a Japanese warrior doll with long red hair and a fierce scowl glowering in the dining room—but from the outside, it looked like any other, on the driveway my father's Impala parked beside my mother's Valiant.

In school I'd been teased for eating raw fish, sushi not yet a craze across America, and it's true that we ate rice, tofu, miso, and tempura as well as sashimi, that we used chopsticks as often as we used forks and knives. But we consumed these meals indoors, and our food didn't leave a telltale odor in the house or my clothes: even as a child I knew to be grateful for that, and we ate steak, too, and roast beef. In the summer we sat out on lawn chairs and my father grilled hamburgers and hot dogs and the neighbors dropped by, and as the fireflies rose like embers from the grass, my sisters and I toasted marshmallows that we shared with the neighborhood kids.

Looking back now, though, I can see that we overcompensated, as visitors and new immigrants do. Less than a year after we'd returned from Japan, my father took me to Kmart and bought me a Fourth of July outfit, a red sleeveless shirt and blue shorts with stars. One Christmas I remember bedecking myself in red and green and—could it be?—draping tinsel in my hair. So maybe that's why one Halloween some teenagers assembled outside our house, special chalk in hand. We reeked of desperation, of eagerness to fit in.

Or maybe it wasn't only racism. That would explain why we were targeted, and our Chinese American neighbors weren't. My mother had mentioned stick figures: glancing through our windows as they wandered past our house late at night, maybe the teenagers had spotted my father in his underwear or the flowing women's nightgowns he liked to wear. Maybe they heard the shouts and screams, the overturning of furniture, the crash of bodies hitting the floor. Maybe they remembered the wail of the siren slicing through dinner conversations, the police car spinning red and blue lights in our driveway.

No, that's being too kind. That's giving the street defacers too much credit. They hated us because of who we were, because our hair was black, our skin yellow, our eyes slanted, our names strange, because according to the mean kids at school, we ate *flied lice* and *rived* on a *load*.

And even if I can't recall the words painted in front of our house, I have my own memories. High schoolers throwing snowballs at my mother and calling her *Chinee* outside the mall late one night, after we'd been to see *Star Wars*. When we arrived at our car, my older sister's friend—her name was Janet, which seemed perfect, so American was she, so big and busty and blond—dusted the snow off my mother's shoulders and back, clucking her tongue, as my sisters and I avoided each other's eyes; we never did discuss it.

Or another time, our first outing as a divorced family, when my mother, flushed with pride after she'd started working in New York, took my younger sister and me to her scene of triumph, and oh the irony, right by the Statue of Liberty a man began screaming at us. My mother gathered us together and we turned around, trying not to run, followed, thank God, only by his shouts. *Fuck you, go home, Jap Commie bitches.*

But this kind of racism, ugly and overt, probably wouldn't have affected my father's career, not at a university. I recall then a rumor I heard at a prior college I taught in: how in a job interview, a Korean American candidate's "quiet ways"—a description that my source deemed suspect in itself—had been attributed to her deferential Asian personality. Not her fault, the committee had said, but this isn't the right place for her.

It's then that I realize my error. I've been on the lookout for out and out bigotry, slurs, hatred, and discrimination at work, when what I'm searching for is more slippery.

A few years back, while adjuncting at another college, I fell in with a group of friends who'd been teaching there for years. Most were tenured, august scholars and artists, but W, a songwriter, was a moonlighter like me. While the others were older by fifteen years or more, W was my age, and funny and bright. Her cubicle wasn't far from mine, and we spent our office hours chatting and gossiping. I was single. Although W was with a musician, a woman, their relationship was long-distance: our evenings were our own, and we often went out for dinner or drinks.

Months passed before I realized that W wanted something more than friendship. I was still waiting for an opportunity to tell her that I didn't feel the same—dear to me though she was, I liked men—when another member of the circle, let's call him Benny, invited W and me out.

We were at a bistro near our college—crowded, noisy, and hip; banquette seating, W and I on one side—and on our second round when Benny cocked his head. "You two look good together," he said.

I tensed. He was drunk, that was obvious, his voice loud, the words slurred.

Benny told me to look at W. "Isn't she beautiful? Isn't she funny and charming?" he said. "Don't you like her, Mako?"

It was an ambush. I wondered briefly if it had been planned, but when I turned, W was red-faced, pooling with embarrassment.

I told Benny that he was mistaken. W was my friend, and that was all.

"C'mon, kiss her, Mako," Benny said, waving his glass, wine slopping over the edge. "You know you want to."

On the verge of walking out, I stopped myself. Benny was good-hearted, and he'd been the first to befriend me at the college: I owed him. I steeled myself, forcing a smile, and eventually managed to change the subject.

Half a year later, at the tail end of summer: I'm at a dinner party in the backyard of a lavish summerhouse owned by a classicist in the department. Also in attendance are a nonfiction writer and Benny and his wife. All of them have met my latest boyfriend, an architect, and the incident with W seems a long time ago; I'm startled when Benny brings it up. He needs to apologize, he says. He'd had too much to drink; he hopes I can forgive him.

Our host—elegant and patrician, a well-known scholar I look up to—chimes in. It was her fault. She says that over a series of long phone conversations, W had confided that she had feelings for me. W had been so sure I reciprocated her affection that the host hadn't questioned it. The host had relayed the news to Benny, and, well, *voila*.

When the nonfiction writer nods knowingly, air leaves my chest. She's my closest friend in the group and we've spent the greater part of the past three years gabbing about past sexual escapades. Surely she couldn't have thought I was closeted, out of touch with my own physical needs and heart?

Before I can find the words, they're all speaking. They hadn't known what to think. But in the end, the host's certainty had won them over. Of course they know now that they were mistaken.

I hesitate. All four of them are watching me, their faces, lit by the moon and the guttering candles on the table, concerned. Penitent.

Their misapprehension smarts. Yet when I come up with the proper words about water under the et cetera, I find that I mean them. They've known and loved W for years. Why should they have trusted me, the new girl, over her? They've been warm, gracious, and oh so kind to me. I'm fortunate to have their friendship.

Later, as the evening is ending, I cart dishes into the house. I'm drying my hands in the kitchen when the host enters with a tray of glasses. After setting it down, she comes up to me and says again that she's sorry.

The room is dark, lit by only a single lamp in the corner. Drifting in from outside is a cool breeze and the sound of laughter, words, and the clinking of glasses and silverware.

I say again that it's fine. Although, I add, I was surprised: if I couldn't admit or even know my own desires, in this day and age, when we're in one of the most liberal professions, and in a town where women can kiss in public—well, how sad. Wouldn't that be a sorry state.

The host says that when I hadn't responded to W's overtures, they'd all talked it over and wondered briefly if W could have misread the cues.

But in the end, she says, *we decided it was cultural.*

Standing in the shadowy room, I swallow. I have a suspicion about what she's suggesting—Asians are repressed; we're uptight, overly cerebral, inscrutable even to ourselves—yet I can't believe it.

What do you mean? I ask.

We thought you couldn't admit how you felt, she says, *because you're Japanese.*

Stung into directness, I say that I'm American. *A Jersey girl, born and bred.*

Even so, the host says.

I feel my jaw clench. But not until years later do I ask myself why I didn't think of my father then: why I didn't remember how he raged and railed against America's racism, why I didn't add one and one to come up with two.

WHEN TOJO
CAME TO VISIT

A year and a half after my father's death, when I'm in Tokyo, I meet with a school friend of his, the writer of the condolence letter that my older sister read at the memorial.

The friend, a short fat man in a wheelchair, brings out photo after photo of black-haired boys in slim-fitting navy school uniforms, his pudgy index finger darting out to find my father. The tall lean one in the back of the class picture, there. That boy in the jaunty cap, grinning between two of his friends. The kid swinging from the tree off to the side. *Look at that smile.*

When the friend starts in on my father's academic achievements—his uncanny early brilliance at math! the highest scores in the country on the University of Tokyo entrance exam! the national outpouring of pride about his MIT fellowship!—I should tune out. It's old hat for me and a buzzkill besides, my father's early promise throwing into relief the disappointment of his later failures. But maybe because of how earnest his friend is, caught up to the point that at times he forgets he's talking of the past, I'm spellbound. I feel as if I'm hearing about a stranger, someone I've never met but always wished to.

Watashitachi-no eiyuu datta, the friend says. *Your father was our hero.*

He tells me that because their school was close to the emperor's palace, important government figures often dropped in on their class. One not infrequent guest was Tojo, the prime minister who gave the orders to bomb Pearl Harbor, starve and massacre millions of civilians, and conduct medical experiments on POWs and was eventually convicted and hanged as a war criminal. During one of his visits, the teacher asked the class what they wanted to be when they grew up. The students were eight years old. The war was in full swing, patriotic fervor at its height. The teacher went around the room, and the students all said soldier or government minister.

"But your father," the friend says, and does his breath hitch there? "Your father stood up and in front of Tojo, he announced he was going to be a scientist."

CLOTHES MAKE THE MAN

It's hard for me to recall it now, and harder still to believe, but in the years before my mother packed us up and fled his house under police protection, my father used to take me flea market shopping, excursions that I looked forward to and loved. I was young then, six or less, his bipolar disorder had yet to manifest, and he wasn't beating my mother badly, or at least not often. He and I would check out the books sections, and then he'd head off to rummage through kitchen supplies while I lost myself among the vintage clothing, an experience that comes back to me now as the smell of mothballs and old perfume and the feel of bristly fur, warm leather, and crinkly, springy taffeta.

Now I dress like my mother, in sleek jackets and pencil skirts, but maybe those outings left their mark. I can't resist the touch of fine fabric—cashmere, linen, silk that slips through my fingers. Yet on that bright February afternoon a decade and a half ago, I was clad in a coarse rayon blazer and matching skirt, nylons, and cheap pumps: an outfit I'd worn regularly years earlier, when I moonlit as a twentysomething paralegal, but that made me feel that day like a counterfeit adult.

The directions I'd scrawled on scrap paper led me to the outskirts of a smog-choked New Jersey city. A few more turns after that, and I was pulling into a huge empty lot. At the far end was a building, gray and squat. If it weren't for the small sign displaying the name of the institution—no mention, of course, of mental health—I wouldn't have believed this was it.

It was just past noon. When I stepped through the double doors, I was surprised to find myself not in a reception area but a lounge, undersized, overheated, and unoccupied except for four men sitting around a table. Dressed in sleeveless undershirts and tees and, though I couldn't quite see and didn't want to stare, what looked like underwear, they were playing poker.

Tucked into a corner was a reception desk, with no one behind it, and on the desk sat a bell, which I rang. I could feel the poker players watching me.

Behind the reception was a tinted glass door, and through it I could make out the outline of a woman on the phone. She held up a finger to me. *One sec.*

As I waited, my eyes fixed on the woman, one of the poker players asked who I was here to see.

Reluctantly I turned. "My father," I said.

The man, dark-skinned and maybe in his fifties, in a stained white undershirt—he was clearly the group's leader—asked my father's name.

"Shoichi," I said. "Shoichi Yoshikawa. He was brought in just two days ago—"

"Sho-chi?" the leader said, his voice cracking at the end. His eyes had widened. "You Sho-chi's daughter?"

Mutters and headshakes from the other players.

I was tense and preoccupied, but almost laughed.

My father was in his sixties then, still working, although the university was doing its damnedest to nudge him into early retirement. He was almost certainly wandering around now in his getup of choice, naked but for a pair of peekaboo boxer shorts. I was in my thirties, living in Manhattan and working as a visiting professor, and the day before, after our nuclear physicist neighbor phoned to tell me that my father had had another breakdown, I'd called my sisters and mother, packed, and stopped at the local Hertz. I dispatched the drive in record time, stopping only near the end to pull into a gas station, change into my paralegal attire, and reapply make-up. To judge from the players' reaction, I'd overdone it, but I always dressed formally when I went to see my father, and I'd assumed this would be an institution like the one I recalled from back in Princeton, when I was a child: hushed and high-ceilinged with shuffling, cardigan-garbed WASPs trailed by attendants, less *One Flew Over the Cuckoo's Nest* than first-class airport lounge. Unconsciously I'd imitated what my mother used to wear to visit my father there.

The receptionist, who was also in a tee, came out then. I identified myself, and she said she'd send out my father right away.

As she disappeared through the glass door, the leader said, as if arriving at a well-considered conclusion: "Sho-chi, he all right."

Grunts of assent from the men.

"He wear a dress, but he all right."

A pause. Then another round of grunts, noticeably fainter.

I wondered for a moment if the leader meant a literal dress. But that had just been a phase, and decades ago. *He wear a dress* was probably code for the effeminacy of Asian men, that old racist stereotype.

Then the automatic door at the end of the room opened with a pneumatic whoosh, the poker players and I turned, and my father strode out in a long, baby-blue sundress edged with lace.

When I first saw my father in women's clothes, I was twelve, a gawky girl in pigtails. It was dark, and in my memory the house was quiet in a way that suggested it was very late, my mother and sisters asleep. I must have stayed up late reading again.

I saw him from the back, down the hall. Dressed in an ankle-length, flowered nightgown, he was on his way to his and my mother's bedroom. The hallway was lit, and he wasn't far from where I stood, close enough that I could make out the pattern, small pink roses against a background of white. Made of a wispy, almost see-through material, the gown floated up at the ends with the currents stirred by his gait. It had puffy cap sleeves that hugged his shoulders, and an elastic, scooped back neckline that exposed and emphasized how his hairline came to a sharp point at the center of his neck.

I felt physically sick. What would the mean girls at school say if they found out?

By that point I was rarely talking to him. But the next morning, when he was drinking scotch and rereading Asimov in the living room in his boxer shorts, I marched up and asked why he'd been wearing a dress.

He looked up. His body was pale and skinny, but his stomach stuck out, round as if he were with child.

"Dresses are prettier than pants," he said, crossing his thin, hairy legs. "They make me feel pretty."

Baffled and irritated, I glared at him. "You're a *man*," I said. "You're supposed to want to look handsome, not pretty."

If he had an answer, I can't recall it. But he laughed, I remember that, the ice in his glass clinking as his belly heaved.

Half a year after my father's death, I start to wonder about his cross-dressing. Why was he drawn to women's clothes? Was his desire to wear them related to his unhappiness—was he upset at having to dress like a man, or maybe even because he secretly wished he was a woman?

I hit the books first. Novels, memoirs, psychology articles, accounts culled from chat rooms, a coffee table book on men in skirts. They make it clear that there's not just one reason that men wear dresses. I read about cross-dressers who are trying out a permanent transition; like to pass as girls for the day; revel in looking like men while rocking halter tops, minis, lipstick and fake lashes; pull on thongs for sexual stimulation; or slide into skirts for comfort, ease, or style.

An array of reasons, any of which could apply to my father.

From old prewar photos that I found after his death, I know that when he was young, his grandmother, nannies, and nursemaids had dolled him up in elaborate outfits, ornate kimonos as well as a sailor suit, complete with matching hat. So maybe he missed being dressed up, the fun of becoming someone else. Maybe nightgowns and sundresses felt less restrictive, kimono-like.

Or was wearing women's apparel erotic for him? Had he urged his girlfriends and wives—my mother!—to let him wear nightgowns during sex? With all the girlfriends he'd had, not to mention the specificity of the porn I found in his bedroom drawer after his death, naked, plus-size women in coy poses, I couldn't quite believe that he liked men, but of course it was possible.

Or maybe he, macho and sexist, given to snide remarks about women's brains around my mother, sisters, and me, had wanted to be one of us all along.

Clothes can be, perhaps in the modern world always are, Darwinian. Just as cuttlefish change colors to blend with their environment, outfits serve as camouflage, costumes to help us fit in; pass racially, culturally, and socially; and hide. When my father wore traditionally masculine duds, the suits, ties, and pants he'd needed for work, maybe he felt like he was in drag. Maybe only in a dress had he felt truly himself.

Clothes can also serve as an adaptive strategy: a means of self-protection, of intimidation. Even now, my tiny, slender mother clings to the linebacker shoulder pads she and other women wore in the 1980s. No matter what I tell her about modern silhouettes, she—whom my father used to drag around the house by her hair, whom he pulled toward the stove, the blue flames coming up with a whoosh as the smell of burnt hair filled the kitchen—insists on snipping off the shoulder pads from her old jackets and stitching them on to the new. In one of the few visits I paid my father in his final decade, I wore Doc Martens, the toughest, meanest boots I owned. Made of black patent leather, they had four-inch heels, thick and sharp-edged enough to bash a man's skull in, and a gratifying heft. In them I felt powerful, a cobra rearing up and spreading its hood. As I clomped around his house, the very furniture quaked.

When Rob and I cleaned out my father's house a couple of months after his death, Toshiko-san pleaded with us to get rid of his dresses before anyone saw them. So when I phone her to ask about them, I'm unsure how freely she'll speak.

"*Yada ne*," she says—*Yuck*—and I know that behind her always-smudged bifocals, she's making a face. "I say to him why you *do* that." She says it wasn't just dresses. He also wore women's shirts. You could tell because they were buttoned on the wrong side.

"What about shoes?" I ask.

"No women shoes," she says. "Never." Then, unexpectedly, she chortles. "Underpants. He wear women underpants."

I think of lacy underwear over a pair of pale, hairy legs. Or would my father have gone for satin? "Does that mean—" But the words—*Did the panties excite him?*—jam in my throat. Instead I say, "Do you know when he wore them? If he saved them for special occasions or, or if—"

"All the time," Toshiko-san says. "He wear them all the time."

"Was he wearing women's clothes when he died?"

"When he die," Toshiko-san says, "he *naked*." The last in a stage whisper.

"That can't be. The cop who called me never said—" I break off. Of course the cop didn't say anything. Why would he, when his only task was to notify me of my father's death. My father hated wearing clothes. It adds up.

"In his room," Toshiko-san says, "women clothes everywhere. Dresses, underpants, nightgowns, shirts."

I'd imagined Toshiko-san and the neighbor's son whose help she'd sought entering my father's bedroom to find a scene of desolation: the bare room with the streaks on the walls from the ceiling leaks, my father's pale body, the smell. Yet if skirts, nightgowns, and women's underpants of all colors were strewn about on the floor, sliding off the dresser, and hanging on the chair like banners—well, the scene was less grim than I'd thought.

"I didn't see any women's clothes there," I say.

"Because I *hide* them," Toshiko-san says. "I hide them before the policeman come."

Now we're both laughing. "You didn't," I say, but it's all too believable: Toshiko-san scurrying around to toss the dresses into the closet when the neighbor stepped out to phone the police.

When I met him, the cop had grilled me about Toshiko-san—who she was to my father, why she was checking up on him, how she'd gotten the keys to his house—and I'd thought, bristling, that he was suspicious of her because she was Japanese, because she, like my father, spoke with a strong accent. Like so many cops, he was racist. Why else would he target Toshiko-san, so neat and proper in the navy blazer and pants she wore like a uniform? But if said lady had been flushed and out of breath when she opened the door, if on her open face the cop read guilt, worry, and fear, the answer was obvious.

"One last question," I say. "When you asked my father why he wore dresses, did he have an answer?"

I can feel her shrug through the line. "He say they better, that's all."

Later that day, when Rob and I sit down for dinner, I tell him what Toshiko-san said. He's been interviewing for college admin jobs, which requires suits, but he abides by the hipster-prof handbook otherwise, sticking to dark tees, suit jackets, and jeans. Still, he cares about clothes, and I ask if he remembers what my dad was wearing the one time they met.

A button-down shirt and pants, he says, corroborating my memory. No, he didn't notice which side the shirt was buttoned on.

I look down at my plate.

"You okay?" he asks.

"I don't even know what I'm looking for," I say.

He could remind me how often he used to ask what I hope to find regarding my father—and how I'd finally blown up, yelling at him that I knew what I was doing; couldn't he just leave me alone? But he just nods.

"When we were cleaning out your dad's house," he says, "there was so much stuff everywhere, scissors and computers and thumbtacks."

He begins clearing the table.

"More than anything else, though," he says, "there were women's clothes. Closets stuffed with housedresses and coats, boxes of suede skirts and shoes, and who knew the world had so many different kinds of polyester florals?"

I pantomime my mind exploding.

"Right," he says. "It never occurred to me he was buying all that stuff for himself."

I wait.

"So when you told me about the cross-dressing, it required a pretty major shift on my end." He shakes his head, smiling. "I had to go back and resee what I saw."

"And?"

"I saw your father was more rational than I'd realized," he says. "More purposeful, less captive to a bargain or hoarding compulsion. Less—" He smiles again, apologetic. "Well, less crazy."

My memory of my father in his nightgown is crystalline, among the sharpest of my childhood. So I'm nonplussed when I call my mother to ask about his penchant for women's wear and she doesn't know what I'm on about.

"He didn't do that when he and I were married," she says. "That must have started later."

"Oh no," I say. "Don't you remember, he used to wear night-gowns—"

"Nightgowns? I don't think—" Then, suddenly, she's laughing, peals of laughter bright as chrome. "You're right. I remember him wearing a pink one once."

Obviously I'm glad that my mother is climbing out of the funk, the morass of guilt, regret, and grief that she's been foundering in since my father's death. But his yearning to dress as a woman and his need to hide it—is that really a laughing matter?

"I remember at least a few times," I say stiffly, "so more than once."

She's still chuckling. When she finally quiets, I try again. "Did he—" Did he wear nightgowns during sex? But close as we are, I can't ask her *that*. "You don't think he liked men, do you?" I say.

"You mean because he wore women's clothes?" She sounds surprised, even a little amused. "I didn't know the two went together. But I'm sure he liked women."

I suppress a sigh. Her response confirms what I'd thought. But

I'm tiring of how everyone, including my seventysomething Japanese mother, seems to know more about cross-dressing than I do.

"What seems strange," I say, "is that he never seemed to like clothes."

"He didn't." Her voice is solemn again. One time during a breakdown, she says, he'd been so frantic to get out of his clothes that he began screaming and crying as he clawed at them. They seemed to be burning him, causing him physical pain. She wanted to help: if he hadn't been thrashing about so much, she would have cut his pants off.

"Then he ran out into the snow, almost naked," she says. "That was one of the times he was hospitalized for months."

We're both silent.

"Actually," I say at last, "I meant he never seemed interested in fashion."

"That's true," she says. I can hear the smile in her voice, and I know that she's recalling the cheap shirts, Kmart flip-flops, and boxer shorts in the flimsiest material: memories softened by time and his death.

"He never cared what he wore," she continues. He always grabbed whatever was closest, even if it was lying in a heap on the floor, and so what if he put it on inside out or backward? "He was a typically absentminded scientist that way."

My mother loves getting dressed, as I do, her closets lined with dresses and trailing skirts in crimson, emerald, and sapphire blue. She's censorious about what other people wear, holding me over the fire for my fealty to black. But in her voice now is a note, faint but unmistakable, of admiration, and I know that to her my father's sartorial indifference was yet another mark of the purity of his mind.

"Was his cross-dressing related to how he wanted to strip off his clothes?" I ask. "Something he did when he was sick?"

My mother hesitates. "I never thought so, but I guess that could be right."

As I'm hanging up, two thoughts bob up in my mind.

The first: that in the last years of our father's life, both my sisters, even the older one, had gone to see him more than I.

The second, seemingly even more random, is about the Doc Martens I'd worn to my father's. How they—patent leather, after all!—gleamed.

Before that visit I hadn't seen him in two years, maybe more, and when he opened the door and took in my shearling and shiny Docs, his eyebrows rose. Then his expression had shifted to one I recognized from my childhood. A foolish, ingratiating grin, one he wore when he was around American adults and felt lost, unable to follow the conversation or get their jokes.

"You look so grown-up," he said.

I felt a flash of irritation. He'd overstepped. I can't recall what I said in response. *Well, I am 37*—was that it? *No shit* was just a thought, I'm almost certain of it, words left unsaid.

But he flinched, I know that, his grin slipping.

Barely an hour has passed since my call with my mother. She picks up on the second ring.

"I didn't know him," I say. "I never—" I stop, unable to continue. *I never tried to.*

She must know, because she always does, how close I am to tears. Yet what I get is her stock response to all my tough questions about my father, this time uttered so firmly that mired as I am in despair and regret, I know with the clarity of truth that she'd recited it to herself, mantra-like, with increasing fervor and diminishing faith over the course of their twenty-four-year marriage.

"He was sick."

Not until days later do I get it. The question isn't why my father wore dresses, but why I'm bothered that he did. If both my mother and Toshiko-san—women who'd come of age in 1940s Japan!—could laugh about my father's fashion choices, if the poker players, tough guys, weren't fazed, why does it worry me?

It's not the cross-dressing itself. When I first saw my father in a nightgown, it was the late seventies. Cross-dressing seemed the province of drag queens and sex workers, and homophobic slurs were a constant in the playground and the world beyond. I was on the cusp of adolescence, confused and miserable about the changes my body was going through. Perhaps inevitably I felt mortified. And yes, the truth of it is that I feel a little squeamish, even now, imagining my father's arousal as he rolls a pair of pantyhose up his legs—but the issue is more about his arousal than the pantyhose.

We're in the second decade of the twenty-first century. My male students sport nail polish and my female ones don spats. I don't mind that my father wore dresses—in fact I'm glad that in a life seemingly devoid of simple as well as deeper joys, he derived pleasure from a nightie with puffed cap sleeves.

What bothers me is the *reason* I don't know why he cross-dressed: I didn't know him. I cut him out of my life.

When I dig out the Docs I'd worn to visit my father and lace them up, they're as I suspected, less tough than I remembered. What distinguishes them is how they draw attention. The heels thunk. The patent leather catches and reflects the light.

For years I'd told myself that when I went to visit him, the finery

I wore was armor. It was a warning. I was an adult and an American, cognizant of my rights and privileges. I could summon resources. He couldn't hurt me any longer and shouldn't try. Yet the truth was that I wasn't in danger from him. I hadn't been for years. I always had a getaway car parked in the driveway, ready to spirit me away at the first sign of trouble, and by then he was frail, eroded by his age and decades of illness and meds, and lonely and eager to please rather than confrontational. I didn't need protection. Nor did I wear the nice clothes for comfort, to bolster my spirits. Sure, when I made my getaway, I burned rubber, tripping speed traps and racking up tickets. But I wasn't like my older sister, who until the end, even when our visits with our father couldn't have been less dull, wept and couldn't sleep for days after seeing him.

No. The way I dressed on my visits was less about my father's beatings than his Kmart flip-flops, thick accent, and foreign ways.

The uptown garb, the shearling and gleaming boots, I put on were meant to draw a line between him and me. As unthinkingly cruel as any middle-school mean girl, I wore them as a signal, to put him on notice, never mind that he'd received the message long ago. I was my mother's daughter. Not his.

THE PROMISE

He swore he'd get me a pony. A shiny new bike. A sailboat. A house on the beach. A jeep. A trip around the world. According to my mother, I needed to ignore those promises. They were a symptom; he was sick. By the time I was a teenager, I knew she was right. But when I was nine and my father promised me a jungle gym, I didn't know any better. When we talked about where the gym set would go, I jumped up and down and cartwheeled with excitement.

Within the week, he came home with the pieces, metal poles in primary colors and a set of big boxes. He fetched load after load from his Impala while I ran around underfoot. He was at it for less than an hour before I lost interest. I ran inside to watch the *Brady Bunch*, turning up the sound to drown out the hammering.

By the morning of the third day, it was finished. The biggest jungle gym in the neighborhood, it had a ladder, a high metal swing, a slide, a set of rings, monkey bars, and a heavy rope with a big knot at the end.

I played on it for years, clambering up the rope until my palms were raw, hanging upside down from the swing, and whispering with friends on top of the monkey bars, our scabby legs swinging free. That first summer I almost spent more time on it than off. One evening I turned around and saw my father through the glass door. I called out to him, and he came outside and watched as I swung myself hand over hand to the end of the monkey bars. The sun had set, fireflies sparking upward, the air scented with honeysuckle and our neighbors' barbecue. My father was a slim dark shape, barely distinguishable from the trees. When I reached the end of the bars and jumped down to the ground, he clapped.

PRESSURE EQUALS FORCE DIVIDED BY AREA

On a wintry night a month and a half after my father's death, my cat Miranda begins to scream and convulse. She's eighteen, her kidneys are failing, the cancer has spread from her lungs to her brain, and two weeks have passed since the vet said *Any day now*: I think I'm ready. Yet after the long midnight drive through snow and ice, Rob fighting to keep the car steady as I struggle in vain to keep Miranda calm, the dash into the hospital, and the shot that makes her eyes shut and her body go limp and quiet in my arms, I start sobbing and can't stop for what seems like days.

She was my second gray tabby and the cat of my single years, and months later I still grow teary talking about her. Friends, even those with beloved cats and dogs of their own, exchange glances, murmur sympathetically, and change the subject to the shock of my father dying the day before Rob's and my wedding. *Now that was a lot to handle. How was the memorial, anyway?* Their concern is a comfort, and for months I'm too worn out to mind that they assume that unbeknownst to myself, I'm grieving not for my cat but my father. But by April, when the two new kittens, wide-eyed, angel-faced hellraisers that Rob and I have gotten to fill the emptiness of our house, are finally settling in, the idea has wormed its way under my skin and started to fester.

When my family returned to New Jersey after two years in Japan and I began school, I was nine, and friendless but for my cat. He was mine because he'd chosen me, to my astonishment, over my sisters. He was gray and striped and I named him Kumo, "cloud" in Japanese.

As the days grew shorter and the weather began to turn, I started smuggling Kumo inside the house against my father's orders. One night, while passing by the bedroom I shared with my younger sister, my father spotted him nestled in the covers of my bed. With a roar he rushed in. I was cowering—he'd already hit me for bringing Kumo inside, two times very badly—but this time he snatched the cat up and gripped him around the throat.

My sister screamed. Kumo, his body dangling, let out a yowl that turned into choking sounds. His paws scrabbled at the air. I was crying, begging my father to stop. Kumo's bladder loosened and the smell of his piss, biting and acrid, filled the room. But my father held on, so tightly that his arms were shaking, long enough that I went from dreading the moment Kumo's body would go limp to wishing for it.

Instead my father dropped him. Kumo righted himself, stumbled, and half ran, half staggered for cover under the bed. His voice quiet, my father said that I must never do that again, and then turned and left the room.

Afterward, Kumo was different. Though built like a bruiser, with thick shoulders, he had a gentle soul. A born loafer, he loved nothing more than to loll in the sun with me at his side. Yet after that night, he was jumpy and skittish. He ate poorly and groomed himself until he had bald patches. When he heard my father's voice or footsteps he raced to hide himself, shivering uncontrollably. Within a year he'd run away, never to return.

◉

Why hadn't Kumo died when my father choked him? By the time I was a teenager, I'd narrowed the possibilities down to three.

A. My father had been playacting, pretending that he was going to kill Kumo to teach me a lesson.
B. Though determined to kill him, he lacked the necessary strength.
C. He started off determined but changed his mind midway through.

Soon enough, though, even before our mother moved my sisters and me out of our father's house during one of his long trips in Japan, I stopped trying to figure it out. Who cares what he'd been thinking? He was a monster no matter what.

But in the months following his death, when I move, dazed, through a world that seems muffled in cotton, I find myself revisiting the question, and wondering about option C. What if my father had been in the throes of bipolar rage until something—the delicacy of the neck in his hands, Kumo's choking sounds, or my and my sister's cries—started to sink in? If he came to with a start and dropped Kumo feeling shock, horror, or even contrition, then maybe I'd been wrong about him, and he wasn't beyond redemption. Maybe I could forgive him—maybe I could feel pity, if not grief and love.

That night, after Rob and I watched Jon Stewart, I told him that I was going to research cat strangulation.

"If choking a cat isn't that hard," I said, "if it's so easy that no physical limitation could have kept my dad from finishing the job, then chances are he realized what he was doing and stopped himself."

We were entwined on the sofa. Through the open window came a cool breeze and a chorus of crickets.

"I want to rule out option A," I said. "The idea that my dad was in control, that he acted deliberately, is just too chilling, don't you think?"

Rob's brow was furrowed.

I nudged him. "Is this too much? I know I've been going on—"

He shook his head. "It's just that sometimes I wonder if we shouldn't have gone through with the wedding."

"What does that have to do with anything?"

He gave me a look. Then: "You really don't know?"

"No."

"You're feeling guilty about it." Seeing that I still wasn't following, he said, "You're obsessing about your dad, thinking and researching and writing about him all the time, because you feel guilty that we went through with the wedding."

For a second we looked at each other. Then we were both speaking at once.

"I am?" I said.

"Aren't you?" he asked.

Leading only to possible veterinary interventions and grim stories about beloved pets throttled by ex-boyfriends, googling *cat strangulation* is a bust, and after an hour I give up and focus instead on people. I learn on a prosecutors' website that because our necks have little protective tissue, strangling is the most lethal form of domestic abuse.

Four factors determine the efficacy of strangulation. Where the hands are on the neck, how much pressure they apply, how long they squeeze, and how much surface area they cover. The exact location of the hands is especially important, as relatively slight pressure on certain points—the carotid arteries, which supply oxygen to the brain, and the jugular, which conducts deoxygenated blood out of it—can yield swift results: unconsciousness in ten seconds, death in four to five minutes. An adult male handshake exerts 80–160 pounds per square inch, or psi. Blocking the carotid takes 11 psi, occluding the jugular just 4.4.

So why didn't Kumo lose consciousness? My father's hands were more than big enough to fully encircle a cat's neck, and although I couldn't be sure how long he'd been squeezing, it must have been more than a minute. If he'd exerted any kind of pressure, he must have compressed Kumo's carotid and jugular.

Had my father not been squeezing hard? I think back, trying to remember. Maybe he'd been in control all along? When he dropped Kumo, maybe he hadn't been sorry and chastened, but icy calm.

On an unseasonably cool afternoon a week later, I bring Otis, the larger of our new kittens and my third gray tabby, to the vet for a check-up. After finishing with Otis—his weight is off the charts but fine for his length; his teeth could do with the occasional scrub— the vet asks if I have questions. I remind him that I'm a novelist, let him think I'm writing a murder mystery, and ask if he could tell me, for research purposes, how difficult it is to strangle a cat?

The vet folds his arms. He's in his late thirties, a little younger than me. He has a new haircut, one so short it makes him look ascetic, a modern-day monk in blue scrubs and Nikes. Fitting, I'll think later, since what I've come to him for is absolution.

He's lucky, he says, cat strangling isn't something he has to deal with in Cambridge. He'll do his best, but could I be more specific about what I mean by *difficult*?

I explain what I've learned about the carotid and the jugular and a person passing out in ten seconds. Does that apply to cats?

The vet reaches down to pick up Otis, who's jumped off the table and is promenading the room, tail high. Otis lifts his chin to be scratched and the vet, smiling, obliges. Huge and charismatic, a peculiar blend of cheek and zen calm, Otis has a way of taking over a room, and the vet has a soft spot for him. When he pets him, he speaks in an almost-baby voice, one I never heard him use with Miranda.

"This is the jugular," he says, holding Otis by the scruff of his neck and tracing a line down his throat. "It's recessed, so you can't really apply pressure to it. And a cat's carotid is buried too deep for us to see."

My eyes are on Otis. I'm remembering how, even as he struggled, Kumo seemed to tremble in my father's grip, and how I couldn't tell if that was from his fear or my father's exertion or both. "You're saying that it'd be hard to strangle a cat."

The vet nods. "The cat wouldn't pass out for at least thirty seconds, maybe more, and he'd be scratching and biting the whole time."

When he first told me about Miranda's cancer, I'd cried. Rob was there to sweep me up then, but this is different, just the vet and me in the small, sterile room.

"So this is for a novel you're writing," he says.

His voice is gentle. He'd seen both Miranda and me through her decline. I should have known he'd spot my little ruse. Does he wonder if the cats and I are in danger?

"Something like that," I say. Otis's tail is twitching. His eyes are golden, unblinking, and a little wild.

Inside me is a feeling, no maybe that's just an apprehension, that the weariness threatening to pull me under isn't because the vet's words mean that option C is off the table, but because it wouldn't matter even if they didn't. A foreboding that as a child, I'd grasped a truth that I can't face now. *A monster no matter what.*

I can feel the vet's glance. "I know there's evil in the world," he says. "But I'd rather focus on what's good—like this sweet kitty here." His last words in that almost-babytalk voice as Otis, claws flashing and fangs gleaming, flops on his back, tender belly bared.

FORCE EQUALS MASS TIMES ACCELERATION

A family dinner in late September of my fourteenth year. The air was balmy; a triangle of golden light jutted from the window at the far end of the kitchen. A month ago my older sister had lit out for college, so there were just four of us: my father, mother, younger sister, and me.

In and out of institutions, his career in tatters, my father was always angry those days, and that evening it escalated the usual way. He didn't want tomato sauce, he hated spaghetti served that way, how could our mother be so stupid. With every sentence his voice rose, my younger sister shrinking back into her chair and beginning to whimper and cry. Our mother picked at her food and kept her head down, doing her best not to antagonize him even though she could read the warning signs as well as me: she must have known it was futile.

When he lunged at her, he bumped against the table. One of its legs, the one that I'd been secretly kicking at as I ate, had been shaky for some time, and with the impact the screws that bolted it to the table finally came loose. In my memory the table was still level even with the leg gone; it remained suspended in air for a full three seconds before it tilted, and then my father's scotch tumbler and our plates and glasses of Hi-C and water were sliding slowly and then more and more swiftly to the ground, where they cracked, shattered, or coasted on tomato sauce to safety, the spaghetti slithering like worms sprung from a can. By then my mother was screaming, trying to shield herself with her arms on the ground, my father's blows and kicks coming down on her from all directions, and he was yelling and my sister was bawling.

A few months earlier, I'd called the cops on him, and perhaps it was the power I'd felt when he hadn't killed me afterward. Maybe it was just the sight of the table leg, flecked by tomato sauce, rolling back and forth beside the broken plates at my feet. The leg was bowed, thick in the middle and top, but tapered enough at the bottom that even a teenaged girl could almost encircle it with her hands. I hefted it and its weight felt good, substantial but balanced, and then I was up and swinging it at my father, hitting him on the upper arm. There wasn't a lot of force to the blow, not because I held back but because I had no momentum; it had happened so fast, an act of pure instinct, and my grip wasn't firm and in my haste I didn't bring the leg back far enough. But my father staggered, one foot skidding backward on the tomato sauce that seemed to be everywhere: poetic justice, I'd think later, though maybe it was just farce.

Then he was shouting, pulling his arm back in order to strike me. The table leg was slick, and my fists tightened on it as I drew it back to take a real swing at his head and that precious brain of his. I could already feel the satisfying crack of wood against his skull in my palms and arms, the way the blow's force would make the table leg kick back, the wood humming in response. Yet my father, in his mid-forties, was already old. Half-blinded with rage and tears though I was, I suddenly saw that. His chest was sunken, his stomach swollen; his limbs were skinny, his balance poor and his reactions slow; he was prematurely frail, his medication and months-long hospital stays with his wrists and ankles in restraints and, who knows, maybe even the deprivation he'd suffered as a child in wartime Japan catching up to him, and as the years passed he'd grow weaker and more and more unsteady while I'd be stronger, tougher, and, I thought as I faced him, with any luck, meaner.

I dropped the table leg and, using both hands and all my strength, pushed him in his chest. My father stumbled and tottered backward. He almost righted himself, but call it the revenge of the tomato sauce: at the last second, he slipped and fell.

The story I want to believe in—the one I'd been telling myself for years, all the way up to and even a few months after my father's death—is that the swing without momentum that I took and the skull-cracking one that I didn't freed me. That after that, I was fine. Ahead lay years of fierce fights with my mother: afternoon sessions in which I'd hold the edge of the large knife I'd pilfered from the kitchen to the blue lines snaking up my wrist; poor grades in math and science; eating disorders, shoplifting, and unprotected sex with dozens of men whose names I barely knew. But fighting with one's mother is a rite of passage; many teenagers shoplift mascara, stick fingers down their throats, and contemplate suicide; defying the odds, the sex with strangers left me more or less unscathed. After that evening, I kept hitting my father back when he hit me, which didn't mean I wasn't an abuse victim, but it made me feel like less of one. My mother, who got us away from him a year and a half later, and her second husband, a very different kind of father and man, did the rest.

Yet every time I enter a shop to return a shirt or earrings or a pair of shoes, I experience a kind of doubling. I'm me and also an other-me, a girl with blotchy and tear-streaked cheeks, a swollen and bleeding bottom lip, and a cheekbone that's turning the colors of a sunset. Someone who's choked with tears and can't speak, an object of embarrassment and horrified pity. A person whom the salesclerks covertly watch as they exchange looks, tut-tutting under their breath.

It's a flashback to some event in my past, that's obvious. I must have bought a sweater or shirt that my father, perennially cheap, had flown into a rage about and made me return. What gets me is that I couldn't have been that young—old enough to walk into a store alone and handle money, tall enough that the salesclerks were close to eye level—and the beating must have been particularly bad: I can recall how my cheekbone ached, my lip stung, my shoulder felt wrenched, and my left leg wouldn't hold my full weight. But these images and sensations float, untethered to any other memory. I can't recall the beating, no matter how often or hard I try.

Still, these are just shards of memory, jagged but slight. Place them and the table leg story on opposite ends of a scale and the shards would fly up in the air, so hard would the table leg side thunk the ground.

So I tell myself I'm fine. Catching sight of a mirror in the store, I say look, there, that woman with the smooth face, dry eyes, and unsmudged makeup, the one by whom a salesclerk, bored but dutiful, waits: that's the only me.

CHESS SUPERHERO

In the summer of his eighth year, my stepfather, Jimmy, taught himself how to play tournament chess from a book. An achievement, to be sure, but one that dimmed beside the scores he'd racked up in his seventy-eight years. So I was taken aback when he phoned to say that with my mother's health more stable, he wanted to take a nostalgia tour of the area surrounding Brandon, Vermont, the site of this self-education. But when he asked if Rob and I would accompany him there for a long weekend, I was all in.

I needed Jimmy's help. Almost a year after my father's death, I was still overcome with guilt and regret, still combing through his life, hunting for the key to his rage and resentment. The search was consuming me. The classes I taught were now a shambles, my marriage neglected, but my father remained a riddle.

The solution was clear. I needed to give up my inquiry. There was no explaining my father. Time to accept that sorry truth and move on.

And if anyone could help me achieve acceptance, it was Jimmy, so sane and serene despite his own troubled parent.

Through MIT's alumni association, my father had become friendly with John Nash, the Nobel-winning genius of *A Beautiful Mind* fame. After meeting him and his wife Alice at my father's memorial, I read up on schizophrenia, the illness that had plagued Nash as well as Jimmy's mother. I learned that because schizophrenia and bipolar disorder both induce hallucinations, disordered thinking, and persecutory delusions, they can be hard to tell apart. To take just one famous case, Zelda Fitzgerald. She claimed to be in communion with Mary Stuart, William the Conqueror, and God. Locked up as a schizophrenic in her lifetime, she's widely considered bipolar now.

Schizophrenia afflicts just 0.5 percent of the population, while bipolar disorder is diagnosed in 2.6 percent, and schizophrenia can be far more severe. Whereas a bipolar episode typically lasts around thirteen weeks, someone with schizophrenia can lose all touch with reality for up to six months, and symptoms of schizophrenia, which include voices in the head that can't be distinguished from real ones, are often dangerous and difficult to live with and manage. My father's friend Nash and Jimmy's old friend and chess buddy, Bobby Fischer, are two of America's more celebrated schizophrenics. There are others who achieved a different kind of fame: Andrea Yates, who drowned her five children in the bath; John Hinckley Jr., who shot Ronald Reagan for Jodie Foster; Mark David Chapman, who murdered John Lennon for Holden Caulfield; and David Berkowitz, a.k.a. Son of Sam, who confessed to killing young, dark-haired women under orders from his neighbor's black Lab.

When I was seventeen, my moods were pinballing, and I was beset once again by the fear that stalks every mental patient's child, I took a chance and went to Jimmy, who'd been in our lives just a month but had already told me about his mother. I asked if he'd ever worried that he'd inherited his mother's illness. He said he'd considered it only to dismiss it, and I asked why.

Because at my core I'm a rational being, he said. *And in case you're wondering, so are you.*

More times and in more ways than I could tally up, Jimmy has saved me. Maybe he could again.

Jimmy likes to tell people he's from Vermont, but aside from summers, he lived there only a year. He was born and raised in Manhattan. His father, Oscar, was a lit professor at City College, one of the few universities that was hiring Jews at the time. His mother was a star student and basketball champ turned housewife. Jimmy's only sibling, Nancy, was born six years after him.

In 1942, feeling troubled by rumors about Hitler, Oscar moved the family up to their Vermont summerhouse. At eight, Jimmy was confident and outgoing. Photos show a boy with a direct gaze and sunny smile. His face was rounder than it is now, but his chin was already firm. He wore his pants hiked high, a habit he maintains to this day.

He was also smart. He'd skipped second grade, and he'd go on to skip eighth and eleventh, allowing him to enroll in college at fifteen. The book he taught himself chess from was almost forty years old, a record of games played at a 1904 tournament. It begins "1 P-Q4, P-Q4; 2 P-QB4" and continues in that vein to the end. Knowing only how the pieces moved, Jimmy deciphered the notations and then played and replayed the moves until he understood the players' strategies.

In a chess game, the first player has twenty possible moves. After each player moves twice, the possibilities expand to almost two hundred thousand; after five moves, over a trillion. In the words of grandmaster Garry Kasparov, "The total number of possible different moves in a single game of chess is more than the number of seconds that have elapsed since the big bang created the universe." A good player can sift through the combinations to determine not only his move but also how his opponent is likely to respond. As a child, Jimmy taught himself how to think up to ten moves in advance.

Reassured that Hitler's reach would not extend to America, Oscar moved the family back to the city after one year. Four years later, at thirteen, Jimmy won the Marshall Junior Championship, a New York chess tournament. At sixteen, he was New York state champion. As a seventeen-year-old Columbia University junior, he was crowned the best college player in the country in the Intercollegiate Chess Championship. He went on to win the US Rapid Chess Championship twice and to finish third in the US Championship three times.

He also attended Columbia Law, married a poet, and defended a convicted murderer pro bono. An idealist from a young age, he surprised everyone in his late twenties by accepting an offer from the corporate world. There he rose quickly. He began trading, another high-pressure activity at which he excelled. He and the poet had three daughters, grew apart, and divorced. He became involved in several charities, donating his time, management skills, and money.

A year after his separation, when he was forty-nine, Jimmy met my mother. Five months later, he'd bought a house in Princeton for us all to live in. Did I mistrust his kindness, love for my mother, or commitment to my sisters and me? Some wariness seems only prudent. Yet as I recall it, I signed on and never looked back. He and my mother had been together just a year, their divorces not yet finalized, when he began introducing me to people as *My daughter, Mako.* No matter how often I heard it, I stood taller.

When he began edging into his seventies, my mother began to worry about him. *He's sad. Maybe depressed.*

I scoffed. She was having flashbacks to her first marriage. Jimmy was the anti-Shoichi. He was older and less energetic, sure. But inside he was the same, a bundle of confidence and good cheer.

In the opinion of no less of an authority than the *New York*

Times, even his chess game was marked by decisiveness and optimism. An article from 1960, when he was twenty-six, noted that the way he played displayed "clear-cut ideas of what he is doing, combined with incisiveness of purpose and a hopeful outlook."

In the program for a qualifying contest for the 1957 World Championship are caricatures of Jimmy, Bobby Fisher, and a Hungarian player. Fisher, crouched over his board with his mouth hanging open, is deep in consultation with a rook and looks simpleminded. The Hungarian, with one perfect curl on his forehead, appears both foppish and coarse. Jimmy, drawn in profile, is handsome and smiling. With his jaw jutting forward, he stands astride his board and rides it as if he were surfing: the poster child for America's postwar ascendance, a chess superhero.

At noon, Rob graciously absented himself so Jimmy and I could talk over a lunch in the sitting room of our inn.

When Jimmy became part of our lives, his mother, Stella, was still alive. My mother met her, but even though I asked, Jimmy wouldn't introduce me. *Too difficult*, was all he'd say. As a result, I know her only through photos: a woman with elegant legs, unfocused eyes, and her son's resolute chin.

Stella had her first episode when she was thirty-eight. For the rest of her life, bouts of psychosis and yearlong hospitalizations alternated with brief spells of lucidity. So when I asked Jimmy over lunch what she'd been like as a mother, I felt thrown when he said she was great. "Very loving and generous, while she lasted."

"While she lasted," I repeated. "You mean, until she died?"

"No, no." He smiled, wide enough that I could see the gap where he'd lost the tooth. "Until she got sick. Then she was accusing me all the time of hooking her up with wires—that hardly qualifies as good parenting."

"But you were just a kid then," I said, "and she lived for decades after that."

"That's right," he said. He popped an olive into his mouth and licked his fingers, placid as a well-fed bear. Was his equanimity about his mother the result of age, time, or personality? Or had he acquired it through discipline and focus?

"Will you tell me about Stella?" I asked.

"Is this about your father again?"

My daughter, Mako. Since my father died, Jimmy had started slipping a *step* into the phrase.

"I think it's about you," I said. "But maybe both."

Sunlight trickled in through the windows. Jimmy had traded the suit he usually wears for flannel and denim. The room we were in had old, braided rugs, needlepoint canvases heralding the joys of home, and a fire dying in the fireplace. On the table beside my pen and notebook were mugs of steaming hot chocolate and assorted delicacies from the enviably good deli in the next town over.

"It was 1943, just after we'd moved back to New York," Jimmy said, "and she seemed to go crazy overnight." One day she was fine; the next she was accusing Oscar of poisoning her eggs and Sanka. The claim that she was God reincarnate, the paranoia about spies who observed her from adjoining roofs, and the assertion that she had a double—she was the false Stella; the real one lived in Connecticut, a wealthy respectable housewife—followed in short order. Two days later, Jimmy came home from school to discover she was gone.

During her first hospitalization, which lasted just short of a year, Oscar buried himself in work. Jimmy was sent to live with Oscar's parents. Their apartment was small—he slept on the sofa—but it was on West 97th Street, half a mile from Jimmy's family's place, so life was not so different. He attended the same school, rode the same bus, and played with the same neighborhood kids. He saw

Oscar every week or two and Stella not at all, and that was okay by him.

"And your sister?" I said, looking up from my notes. "Where was she in all this?"

"I'm not sure," he said, forking stuffed grape leaves onto my plate. "I think she might have been staying with family friends." If the thought troubled him, I couldn't tell.

"She was, what, three years old then?"

"Three or four," he said. "It's incredible, really, how well she turned out. Talking to her, you'd never guess all she's been through."

I couldn't comment, since I'd never met Nancy. I'd long wanted to, but she lived with her husband in the remotest part of Illinois, hours from any airport and surrounded by woods, and Jimmy had made it clear that she wouldn't welcome my presence. Although he made sure to call her once or twice a year, in the decades I've known him, he himself has met up with her just twice. From his stories, I know that she's made a practice of rescuing and taming wild animals, including ducks, pigeons, and even a deer. Photos show her and her husband at supper with the pigeon on her head and the deer looming behind them in the dining room.

"What got me through it all," Jimmy said, "was chess." He'd been serious about it before, but after his mother got sick, he doubled down.

"It was the perfect escape," he said. "It kept me from fretting over circumstances I couldn't change. I've wondered at times what I would have done with my life if I'd had a healthy mother. Growing up in a dysfunctional family, I think I aspired more toward being equilibrated than standing out."

He speared a falafel. "But I have my mother to thank for whatever success I've had with the game."

The fire was just a glow. "So in the end," I said, "Stella was much worse than my father."

Jimmy chewed and swallowed. "I don't think she was a worse parent, if that's what you're asking." She wasn't particularly violent, he said, although she sometimes tried to beat Oscar with a frying pan, and woe betide any hospital staff who let their guard down around her. "She attacked me just once, when I was in my forties."

"Did she hurt you?"

His hesitation lasted barely a second. "No."

I asked about treatment, and he said that she'd had electroshock therapy, that she hated it and called it torture, and that each time, she insisted she would rather die than go through with it again. But the doctors held firm.

"They said it was helping," Jimmy said.

"Was it?"

"I don't know."

He pushed the falafel plate toward me, and I took one, a nutty, spicy mouthful.

"She was also on antipsychotics," he said. "Better than nothing, but not great."

"My dad was on lithium. Also not great."

"Maybe the dosage wasn't correct," he said. "I remember when lithium came on the market. It really works."

I nodded. I'd researched it. When it was first prescribed to bipolar patients in the 1940s, scientists were skeptical. One drug to curb both the highs and the lows of bipolar disorder? Not bloody likely. Evidence of its efficacy quickly mounted, but it wasn't until 1970 that the FDA approved it. By then almost two decades had passed since Edward Teller had used lithium to create the H-bomb, which is fusion-based and as much as a thousand times more powerful than the bombs that demolished Hiroshima and Nagasaki.

To me it seemed a fair match. My father's moods versus a force that leveled cities.

"Lithium worked for my father," I said. "Not when he was

traveling or not sleeping, but for the most part." I paused. "The problem was, he refused to take it."

"That's very common," Jimmy said.

"It might be what I blame my dad for most," I said, surprising myself. It was the truth; I felt sure of that. But why blame him for that when he'd done so much worse?

"It's another symptom," Jimmy said. "Your father denied his illness and rejected treatment and medication because he was sick. Stella was the same."

I felt a flare of irritation. "I don't think that's right," I said.

"It's a well-known phenomenon," he said. "There's a euphoria and a sense of well-being that comes with mania. It feels like the opposite of illness."

"Stella wasn't manic."

"No. But when she was sick, she felt far more well and alive than she usually did. Expecting her to take her medication under those circumstances would have been irrational."

Yes, Jimmy was nothing if not rational. "Still," I said. "It must have made you angry."

His tufted eyebrows lowered. "She was a sad, sad woman," he said. "I was rejected and unloved, but from the beginning, I understood that she was sick. If you understand that, then you can feel hurt, disadvantaged, and underprivileged, but not angry."

"Maybe not angry with *her*," I said. "You could be angry with the world, with life—"

"I blamed her illness," Jimmy said. "I don't think I was angry. Not even with life."

"Even when she died?"

For a moment Jimmy didn't stir. Then he said, "When she died, I felt relief." His voice had deepened. "For the first time, I felt free."

I should have felt surprised, if only because he wasn't as dispassionate as I'd thought. But all I felt was envy. In a couple of weeks, my father would be dead a year. Where was my sense of freedom? Why did I still feel shackled, even trapped?

Maybe the difference was our parents' afflictions. Schizophrenic delusions can be so vivid they're indistinguishable from reality, and they're often terrifying. At their worst, the images and scenarios visited on Stella probably rivaled what was actually happening in Germany when she had her first episode. Whatever she'd done, whomever she'd struck out against, she was acting in self-defense; most courts of law would acknowledge that. That a child could understand that about his mother seemed almost impossible—but Jimmy, brilliant, precocious, and ever so rational, hadn't been just any child. And when his mother finally died, he'd been even older than I was now, with decades of dealing with her behind him.

Or was the difference between Jimmy's and my situations more basic? In very severe cases, like my father's, bipolar disorder is also characterized by bouts of delusion, but more commonly it's milder, and as a result it feels more accessible and understandable to the general population than schizophrenia: it's an illness that many of us can relate to. I know now that many teenagers, even those without bipolar parents, fear that their mood swings have a neuro-chemical basis, whereas schizophrenia, with its voices, visions, and visitations, can seem alien, even uncanny. Those who suffer from it feel more distant, cut off, and beyond our ken.

Even as a child, Jimmy couldn't not have understood that his mother was sick.

"Being schizophrenic is one thing," I said to Jimmy, "bipolar is another." Of course there are similarities and an overlap in symptoms, I said, but if you're bipolar and you have strength, willpower, and a willingness to trust doctors and submit to treatment and meds, you can control and manage the illness. "But there's no drug that's that effective for schizophrenia," I said, "and it's a much worse illness. Your mother was really sick—sick enough that if she was a bad parent, it wasn't her fault. My dad was a different matter altogether."

His brows had inched up. "Your father was really sick, too."

"It wasn't the same."

"I don't think that's true."

"Well, I do."

"I know you know that Shoichi wasn't always how you remember him," Jimmy said. "After all, your mother did fall in love—"

"You know what I know?" I said, my voice loud. "I know I'm tired of hearing about how *he was sick.* I know I hate that people believe he was a victim, like his sickness was some kind of damn get-out-of-jail-free card."

"Oh, Mako—"

But I wasn't finished. "My father," I said, "*he* was violent. Not his illness." I sat back, breathing hard.

The sun had set, and the room was dark and quiet around us. After what felt like a long time, Jimmy sighed and shifted in his chair. "That might very well be right," he said mildly. "But you can't know that for sure."

My investigation into my father's life was founded on a premise: the fact that he was bipolar wasn't the reason he beat us. Should it have been obvious that this premise was flawed? No doubt. But it was a premise I was predisposed to accept.

When I was young, the absence of any external signs of illness—like the rising red of the thermometer or the coughing up of phlegm, as with the flu, or the swollen, hot-to-the-touch joints, as with my mother's rheumatoid arthritis—combined with my father's insistence even at his sickest that he felt fine, better than fine, in fact the best he or any other human being in the whole world had ever felt, made bipolar disorder seem mysterious, elusive, and subject to doubt. That grown-ups used the illness as a reason to make allowances for my father further increased my suspicion that it was something they had made up—a fiction like Santa Claus or those fairytales in which bad children are boiled alive or fed to birds—in order to keep me in line.

After reading up on the illness in my twenties, I could no longer doubt that he had it. Just as Stella's hallucinations about spies and wiretapping matched Nash's, so too did my father's behavior chime with the traits, tics, and predilections I read about in medical articles, memoirs, and novels on his illness. There were the well-known symptoms—mood swings, speech patterns, alcoholism, narcissism, leaps of intuition, delusions of grandiosity, persecutory delusions, explosions of rage, and suicidal tendencies—but also more unexpected ones, like the bursts of generosity and the love of travel. One memoirist noted the sufferer's compulsion to be as high up as possible during manic bouts, a detail that recalled my father's habit of clambering up on the dining table to inveigh against us from above.

So why couldn't I believe that his illness controlled his behavior?

Maybe I wanted to hang on to my anger. Maybe I couldn't bear the thought that my father was nothing more than flawed brain chemistry—I wanted something more interesting, more *narrative*, than a medical explanation.

Or was it simpler? Maybe I was afraid that mine was the story of willful ignorance, a daughter who can't accept that her father was sick.

After lunch Jimmy and I collected Rob, and we all set off for a hike up Blueberry Hill, a small mountain that Jimmy had often climbed as a boy. Thrushes and house wrens sang; the day was bright and brisk, the air sparkling, and the waterfall spectacular. Dreamy with happiness, Jimmy wandered ahead, popping back now and again to regale us with anecdotes about bears, long-ago picnics, his feats of derring-do, and the injuries he'd sustained, while Rob, who was lugging his big camera, set up shots as he muttered to himself about light, focal length, and depth of field. I trailed behind, my eyes on the ground.

We were just past the top of the mountain when Jimmy, falling into step beside me, asked if I was okay, and did I have any other questions about Stella or Shoichi?

I told him no, that I was thinking I'd do more research on bipolar disorder, and that it was all thanks to him. Perhaps it seemed hard to believe, but if he hadn't set me straight, I said, I would have overlooked the impact of my father's illness.

Jimmy said he was glad to have helped, and with a nod, he picked up his pace. But after a few steps, he trotted back to say that I shouldn't feel bad about underestimating the effect of Shoichi's affliction.

"It may be that Shoichi's illness was less apparent than Stella's." He said that Stella during psychosis was markedly different from Stella during her periods of normalcy. As a result, even as a child he could always make a clear distinction between her and her illness. "From what you and Hiroko have said about your father, there was less of a demarcation between well and sick."

Jimmy had always known how to make me feel better.

"It's true," I said. "When I think about my dad now, he seems to blink in and out, so that I can't tell where the bipolar Shoichi ends and the real one begins. Even when he wasn't manic, he acted crazy."

Jimmy was nodding.

"And violent, too," I said. "That happened regardless of his cycles."

He frowned. "I didn't realize that."

I felt a surge that only later I'd identify as hope. "Does that change things?" I said. "Does that mean—do you think his illness wasn't the reason he was violent?"

He gazed ahead, that resolute chin creasing, and I could almost hear his mind, trained to sort through as many moves as the number of seconds since the big bang, sifting through the different possibilities—*clickclickclick* like a thousand abacuses, an insect-like whir.

"No," he said at last. "More probably it's a pattern of behavior. If you're violent during your manic phases, then after a while, violence is normalized. It becomes acceptable, so that later, even when you're not manic, you no longer prohibit yourself."

I heard myself thanking him. Soon he was off again, scouting the trails ahead as I trudged along.

A pattern of behavior rooted in mania. It was the best explanation for my father's violence I'd heard and, let's be realistic, would probably ever hear.

But why, when I'd been searching for precisely such an explanation, did I still feel dissatisfied? Why did I feel even more weighted down, perplexed, and angry?

The answer arrived, crisp and clear as the Vermont air, when I opened my eyes the next morning.

It came down to the question of responsibility. My father's refusal to take lithium angered me, and that anger felt good. It felt clean. That he didn't try harder to get better was something definitive I could hold him to account for, something that was clearly in his control, in contrast to his brain chemistry, moods, temper, or maybe even fists.

But Jimmy was right. I couldn't blame my father for rejecting treatment any more than I could hold him responsible for his violence. Neither was his fault.

The problem was that it wasn't enough for me to stop blaming my father. What I wanted was to *forgive* him. I wanted to understand why he beat and tortured us, and in understanding, to let my anger go.

And if he hadn't been fully accountable for the way he treated us, if it was his illness rather than he that was at fault, then I couldn't truly blame him, but neither could I forgive.

In our inn that evening, Jimmy, Rob, and I gathered in the sitting room with a group of congenial strangers. A fire roared, dinner had been superb, and the wine even better. The conversation, about politics, was spirited, Rob in his element.

Jimmy and I sat off to the side, near the fire. The day had been full, everything that he'd hoped for, and he was tired but content.

"You once told me that I'm like you, rational at the very core," I said. "Do you remember that?"

He shook his head.

"It was years and years ago," I said. "But it's obvious to me that I'm not in the least bit rational, and that I ought to be. My new resolution is to be more like you."

Jimmy chuckled. "That's flattering, but my passion for rationality isn't something to emulate," he said. "There's no doubt that it's excessive, even irrational. A reaction to Stella's psychosis."

"I don't understand," I said.

"I used to try to reason her out of her hallucinations." His rationality, he said, was something he deployed, as both a weapon against her delusions and a defense against her psychosis. He wanted desperately to dissuade her of her craziness, to convince her through logic and reasoning that her delusions weren't and couldn't possibly be correct.

"Trying to talk sense into her," he said, "it was a hopeless pursuit, I know that now, and maybe deep down, I knew that even back then." His smile was rueful. "But I kept trying. I kept fighting with great vigor."

I pictured the boy with the too-high pants. "Even as a kid?"

"Only as a kid," he said. "By the time I was in high school, I knew better."

Talking sense into a schizophrenic: an endeavor so futile it could be an idiom, like tilting at windmills or squeezing blood from a stone.

I'd felt awed that Jimmy, as a child, could accept what I was still struggling with: mental illness controls and dictates behavior; in its throes, a parent is a different person. What I hadn't realized was that Jimmy had apprehended the *fact* of his mother's illness, but not the nature of it—how inexorable it was, how his mother, in its hold, was lost to him, beyond his control and reach.

Beside us, the group erupted in laughter.

Jimmy was talking about how he'd started researching schizophrenia when he was thirteen and how he continued the pursuit in college with a course in abnormal psychology. "I kept thinking I could find a cure or some way around her illness," he said.

By thirteen he had beaten all the young chess players in New York; by college, almost all the adult ones. Was it because of his brains or in spite of them that he'd thought he could cure his mother?

Finding an explanation other than mental illness for my father's violence might be hopeless. But maybe I could forgive myself for hoping, as Jimmy had. Maybe it was okay that I wasn't quite ready to give up on my search.

Another burst of laughter from the group.

Jimmy put his hands on his knees. He was smiling, his face ruddy and eyes bright. "You know, Stella really was a loving, sweet-natured woman," he said.

"I'm sure she was."

"She was ill for so much of her life. But that doesn't mean I don't have good memories."

Drowsy from the heat and the wine, I nodded, stretching.

"In fact," Jimmy said, "all I remember are the good times."

Startled, I turned to look at him. My flannel-and-denim-clad sage, my personal touchstone. The bravest person I knew, able to look a cold, hard fact in the eye; the father I wished I'd had all along. I thought about what he'd said about the poisoned Sanka, the year he'd spent on his grandparents' couch, the spies on the roof, the true and false Stellas, his mother beating his father with a frying pan, and how he'd felt free when she died: were *those* the good times he meant?

But maybe he was telling the truth.

Earlier that day, when we'd driven up to his old summerhouse, we'd found the present owner, an airline attendant in her mid-thirties, out raking leaves. She offered us a tour of the house, with the large, high-ceilinged rooms and wide staircase I recognized from photographs, and afterward Jimmy had stood outside in the luminous autumn light and told her stories of the town in the 1940s. He talked about the Johnsons, whose house was where the yak farm now stood, and the old covered bridges that once lined Otter "Crick" and the magical year he got to spend in Vermont, when his father was worried about Hitler and his mother was not yet ill, and the one-room schoolhouse he attended along with fifteen other children and the stinging cold of the winter mornings and the pails of blackberries he and his mother picked from the hilltops and the hundreds of apples they peeled, cored, stewed, and pounded into applesauce until, finally, he wept. With a warmth that confirmed my sometimes-belief that the kindness of others is not only all we have but all we need, the owner threw her arm around his shoulders, and for an instant I saw him through her eyes—an old man, overcome by longing for a place and people long gone.

MANDALA

It was April, seven months before my wedding with Rob. Four years had passed since I'd seen my father, and when he opened the door, I felt thrown. His hair, iron gray for so long, was a snowy white, and it took a second before I recognized the demon of my past.

All smiles, he greeted me; as usual, we didn't touch. Before I could introduce them, he'd turned to Rob. "You're the filmmaker," he said, beaming. Then, perhaps remembering his manners, he ushered us indoors. "Come in, come in."

In the entryway, Rob and I left our coats on the chair that my father waved toward. As we headed into the living room, I could feel Rob hanging back. Turned off by the state of the house, maybe—the boxes lining the walls, the outdated computers and keyboards littered across the living room. Or was it my father himself, his awkwardness and thick Japanese accent? Despite all my warnings, maybe Rob had thought my father would be like my mother, refined and elegant and assimilated. Maybe he, like other boyfriends, couldn't get over how different my father was from her, or from me.

Our lunch reservation, at a new sushi joint in downtown Princeton, wasn't for another hour. After pushing bowls of M&M's and peanuts at us and asking us twice if we were sure we didn't want drinks, my father, still smiling, settled into the armchair across from us.

"Where's Toshiko-san?" I said.

My father said something about her grandchildren.

"Toshiko-san is my father's girlfriend," I explained to Rob, though he already knew. "I really like her—it's too bad she's not here." I turned back to my father. "Everything okay between you two?" My voice sharper than I intended.

His eyes flickered. "Fine," he said.

I asked if he and Toshiko-san would be taking any trips together, and he said that in October they'd be going on a cruise to Nova Scotia. "We have to drive through Boston to get there. Maybe we can stop by and see you," he said, the last to Rob as well as me.

"Maybe," I said. "Maybe, if we're not away."

"You'll be teaching then, won't you?" my father asked.

I exchanged a look with Rob. "We travel during the term, too," I said. "But give us a call. If we're there, we can do lunch."

Over the phone, my father had told me that his heart condition was getting worse, but he looked well. He was dressed in clothes that fit him, a button-down shirt and slacks. The white hair was becoming, and so was the weight he'd put on—it made him seem more substantial, like a prosperous banker or a sleek pampered cat, and I had the thought that he might live another twenty years.

"You're a professor," my father said to Rob. "Like Mako."

"Like you," Rob said, nodding back at him.

My father grinned. Then, glancing at me: "Two Dr. Yoshikawas right here—"

"No one ever calls me that," I said, "not even my students." My father didn't respond. "I wouldn't want them to," I added.

"Your films," he said to Rob, "they're all different kinds?"

"I told you—" I began.

But Rob was saying that that was right, and my father's face had lit up.

"I'd like to show you something," he told Rob, and then he was leading him, me trailing behind, to one of the computer screens. He pressed some keys and up popped a computer graphic. In Day-Glo pink and orange, it looked like a swirling mandala.

Then he stood back and watched Rob watch the screen. He said, almost shy, "I made it myself."

Even I could tell the work was crude, a throwback to the art video aesthetic of the 1970s, but Rob was nodding. "You wrote an algorithm?" he said.

My father's head bobbed. "Exactly!" he said. "I have others, too." Pulling the keyboard toward him, he began typing furiously. "Let me show you."

Rob was in for it, that was obvious, and with a sigh I sank back down on the couch and plucked a newspaper—the old standby, the *Princeton Packet*—from the pile on the coffee table.

"Oh, this one turns counter-clockwise," Rob said, as another mandala, this one in magenta and green, gyrated on the screen.

My father laughed. "Right again!" he said. "I was thinking that I could show them somewhere. Do you know where?"

I could tell, even if my father couldn't, how little Rob thought of the videos. Did that change how he saw him? He'd only ever spoken of my father with awe—the Princeton professor, the fusion scientist—and through increasingly less subtle hints he'd pushed for this visit, making it clear that even if meeting him before our wedding wasn't a requirement, exactly, it was important. But now, in my father's house, Rob was reserved and almost stilted, a far cry from his usual open and friendly self, and what he'd seen of my father so far—his hoarding, amateur films, and clumsy overtures of friendship—had to be the reason why.

Flipping a page of the newspaper with a snap, I told myself I didn't care. Really, I was glad. It was about time that Rob saw how pathetic my father was, how deluded, still in thrall to his own myth.

◉

We were halfway through our lunch at the sushi joint when I decided that it'd be fine not to invite my father to the wedding. No, it was better. He'd be lost during the festivities in Boston, with all of Rob's and my friends, not to mention my mother and Jimmy. Once Rob and I were married, we'd drive down again and take my father and Toshiko-san out to a celebratory dinner, our treat. And it wasn't as if my father would mind. After all, he and I barely had a relationship. He knew that, how could he not. We both did—so it was strange that I felt a tremor of what had to be nerves before making my announcement. Did I really care what my father thought of Rob?

"I have news," I said.

My father looked up. Always a sloppy eater, he had a grain of rice stuck on the corner of his mouth, and I had to suppress the urge to reach across the table and wipe it off.

"Rob and I are getting married," I said. "Probably sometime this fall."

My father smiled so widely I thought his face might crack. Still the rice stayed lodged in place.

"That's wonderful," he said, nodding at me and then Rob in turn. "Really wonderful. I know you'll be very happy."

It was the last time I'd see him alive. In the months that followed, I'd think many times that of course I'd invite him to the wedding, what's one more person, only to change my mind again. When he left a voicemail, three weeks before the wedding, asking about that lunch in Boston, I'd be mired in party prep and too cowardly to talk, let alone see him, and wouldn't return the call.

After the visit, as I steered our car through the leafy streets of my hometown in the dwindling sunlight, I asked Rob for his verdict on my dad.

Not what he'd expected, he said. "I was on guard, at first."

"Why? You mean—you don't mean you thought he'd attack or hit me."

He shook his head. "Not physically. But I thought he might try to put you down in some way."

For a moment I couldn't speak. "I should have told you. That was in the past."

Rob was looking out the window. "The computer graphics, I didn't expect that either. He wanted to impress me."

Rolling my eyes, I asked why that was news. "He's a narcissist. I know I didn't forget to mention *that*."

"He wasn't doing it to pump himself up," he said. "It's because I'm with you." Then, seeing that I didn't understand: "He wanted to impress me for your sake."

I was about to tell him he was wrong. He didn't know my father. But I hesitated—because my father had been eager to please, because his smile almost cracked his face, or because in spite of everything, in spite of myself, I wanted to believe that Rob was right? I still don't know.

I reached for Rob's hand. We rolled out of Princeton in silence.

TOKYO MONSOON

The trip that I took to Japan in May, to meet with an aunt I hadn't known I had, began eighteen months earlier, with the discovery of treasure: a trove of prewar Tokyo photos in my father's house in Princeton. He'd been dead just three weeks, and I was still unaware of how little I knew of his past.

With my two sisters unable to leave their jobs and families in California, the task of doing a sweep on his house—ransacking it for anything of value—fell to Rob and me. We had to work fast. We needed to get back to our classes in Boston in a couple of days; the liquidator would haul in his dumpster to clean out the house in a week. But our mission would have been daunting no matter what.

After retiring, my father had doubled down on his flea market shopping. His home, an airless, rickety, three-bedroom ranch house, was now a disaster zone. Boxes overflowing with magnifying glasses, pocketknives, pushpins, scissors, baby diapers, and costume jewelry covered the floor and teetered against walls. Crowding the den were two pianos, an electric keyboard, five computers, and four printers.

Then there were our working conditions. My father had died alone in his bed, in an overheated bedroom where water leaked from the ceiling and mold crawled up the walls, and a full day had passed before Toshiko-san discovered his body: a sickly sweet stench permeated the air. I was in constant danger of gagging, and had to step outside more than once for gulps of fresh air.

Rob never needed breaks.

Was he thinking this was a sorry way to start our married life—my father's death, followed by the estate snarl, the planning of the memorial, the memorial itself, and now this, the house with its smell, mold, and clutter? It was a stupid question. Rob wasn't one for self-pity: that was just me.

Given how much more efficiently he worked, it was sheer luck that I was the one to fish out the battered Whitman Sampler's box. I came across it in the bottom of the bottom drawer of a cabinet, buried beneath old prescription bottles and yellowing pamphlets on manic depression. I flipped the lid open. A whiff of what might have been chocolate, and then a stack of old black-and-white photos.

And there my father was, an infant being embraced by a woman with velvety eyes. There again, a small boy in a kimono in an ornate Japanese garden, looking back as if to beckon us to follow. There, a toddler on the lap of an older man with an egg-shaped head, and there, a beatific child encircled by a bevy of young women—maids or nannies, to judge from their aprons—at the seashore.

His eyes were wide-set and alert. His hair was straight and shiny and sculpted into a bowl. He had Dumbo ears, mug handles for the smallest of hands.

In the few prized photos I possess of my mother as a child, she's off to the side or tucked in a corner with a horde of relatives, a tiny kimonoed figure. In these pictures, my father was often by himself, and always front and center. Smiling and cooing, the adults hovered over him—the firstborn! a boy! In one of the most beautiful, he was maybe two, dressed in a formal kimono and standing on a chair. I could see the quality of his kimono in the detail of its design, which was abstract and swirling. The seat he stood on was covered in brocade fit for an emperor's bum.

Other outfits included a sailor's suit, complete with cap; a well-cut shirt and shorts; a dark coat with a furred collar; and other kimonos just as fine. So contented and at home did the boy seem in his fine clothes and surroundings that for a second I thought no way was this my father, only to flip over a picture and see his name printed in bold kanji down the back.

A few photos were taken on the beach, one in what seemed like a park. The rest were all in or set against the backdrop of the largest, grandest old-style Japanese house I'd ever seen. Made out of the traditional dark wood, it had a low, sloping tiled roof, tatami mats, and wide shoji screens. Even by Japanese standards, the garden looked magnificent, complete with mossy rocks, maple trees, and a small pond beneath a gnarled old pine that grew sideways, its branches skimming its reflection in the water.

I took the box to Rob and together we exclaimed. *How much is that kimono worth? Look at him there, like a doll.*

Nothing we'd turned up, not the stamp collection folders, safe deposit key, or gold coins, could compare with this find. Prior to this, the earliest picture of Shoichi I'd ever seen was from his and my mother's wedding, when he was in his twenties: a long-necked young man in a roomy dark suit, smiling a little uncertainly beside his beaming blushing bride.

Not until I was locking the photos in the car for safekeeping did I think about something Rob had said. *It's another world.*

What had he meant? Was he referring to the chasm between 1930s Japan and twenty-first-century America, or to my father's house then and now? The thought made me cringe. I'd come to this cramped ranch house as an infant and lived in it until I was fifteen, and it mortified me. I wanted Rob to picture me—I wanted to picture myself—growing up in the kind of high-ceilinged, light-filled house my mother and stepfather lived in. Not here.

Of course I should have told Rob about my childhood long ago. He needed to know about it—he deserved to. Was he upset with me for keeping secrets? How disappointed was he, how confused?

At the same time, I couldn't help wondering. *It's another world.* If my father's early years had taken place in the fairytale world portrayed by the photos—if he'd been so cherished, surrounded by loving relatives and maids in a gracious, luxurious home—what winding path and wrong turns had led him here, to a lonely death beneath a leaking ceiling in a house crammed with junk?

To hear my mother tell it, my father's life was governed by twists of fate. The luckiest boy in the world—the cosseted son in a family of surpassing wealth, the prodigy with a father and grandfather who could recognize and nurture his brilliance—until he wasn't. First came the death of his mother and then the war years, when Shoichi was sick, emaciated, and always hungry.

After the war, his life resumed what seemed its rightful course. His father remarried; he excelled at his studies. He moved to America, married my mother, began working at Princeton, and started his family.

Then another twist: Shoichi's first breakdown, when he was in his mid-thirties, his three-day-rant about the aliens who'd been chasing him through space, and the months-long hospitalization that followed.

Next came his father's death. As the firstborn son, Shoichi was supposed to inherit the entire estate, which was immense. In Tokyo for the funeral, he discovered that his stepmother had taken advantage of his absence to change the will and diminish his share.

The rest, of course, I knew all too well. His drinking, the escalating violence, the longer and more serious breaks with reality. His divorce from my mother; the second, marginally less miserable marriage that left him a widower. But my sense has always been that even if the wheel had stopped with him on top, a happy life was beyond him. Toshiko-san knew the score. *Your father, never too cheerful,* ne.

◉

Back at home after the visit to Princeton, I fanned out the photos on the dining table. Which ones were Shoichi's parents? The velvet-eyed woman had to be a relative—she appeared too often, and in too many fine kimonos, to be anything else—but was she Shoichi's mother or grandmother? A few different men appeared in the photos, though mostly in just one picture each. I figured that the man with the egg head, who showed up a number of times and often wore Western clothes, suits and sumptuous winter coats and the like, had to be Shoichi's grandfather. Yet where was his father? I asked Rob—from our talk during the car ride home, I knew he wanted to help me research my father's life—and he said he couldn't tell either, but why not give my mother a call?

It was early afternoon, almost time for dinner in England.

My mother was busy in the kitchen. No, she said. She hadn't made any headway yet on the scanned images I'd sent—she still couldn't identify any of the people in the photos, and neither could her older brother, who'd known my father's family well. But she'd keep trying.

I told her that the photos made me see that nature clearly had it over nurture. "To be brought up with such love and care," I said, "and then to turn out so badly." I shook my head.

"Your father wasn't a bad person," my mother said.

He's good inside: I groaned. "Not that old line again."

She sighed. "I know you're still angry." I could hear the sound of sizzling. "Maybe—" She paused and I imagined her standing in front of the wok, her eyes narrowed, the cooking chopsticks forgotten in her hand. "He could be so frightening," she said. "Maybe you can't give him credit for the good times."

"If someone's cruel and violent, I'm not sure it matters if he acts nice once in a while."

Another pause. "What if it was the other way around? Maybe

your father was by nature sweet and loving. Maybe something else, outside of him, came along and made him act badly."

"That's a lot of maybes." I glanced down at the photos on the table, my gaze snagging on a picture of the velvet-eyed woman smiling at Shoichi, circa age four. The woman looked around forty, which had made me think she was probably Shoichi's grandmother, but her smile contained such tenderness, such soft pride and hope, that I suddenly felt sure I was looking at Eiko.

"When you said something might have changed him," I said, "did you mean a childhood trauma of some kind? His mother's death, maybe, or the war?"

My mother hesitated. "Either's possible." Her voice was gentle. "But I was thinking more about his illness. Once his manic episodes started, he really changed."

I stashed the pictures in the lowest drawer of my desk. They were strange, mesmerizing, and in their evocation of a world that no longer existed—the gardens and old wooden houses burned and razed during the war, the kimonos replaced by the wash-and-wear shirts and pants that poured into Japan in the aftermath—poignant. But when it came to the riddle of my father, they couldn't help. In the unlikely event that any of the people in the pictures were still alive, there was no way to track them down. What I needed were the stories behind the images, and those were out of reach.

Almost eleven months later, on the one-year anniversary of my father's death, Toshiko-san and I were standing in front of his grave in the Princeton cemetery. By the time she was finally ready to leave, I was feeling sour.

I shouldn't have come. Not for half an hour of listening to Toshiko-san keen to his grave—*Why you leave me, sensei, where you go*—while I wished I felt something. What made it worse was that I'd ducked out on plans with Rob to be here. He and I already had a hotel reservation for the weekend, but when I told him, with a wistfulness that contained an all-too-clear hint, that Toshiko-san had asked me to accompany her to my father's grave, he'd been patient about shelving our plans. He'd urged me to make the trip, saying, as he had so many times before, that thinking about my father was good for me and, who knows, might even help us, long-term. But I felt guilty about neglecting him again, and sad. After all, the weekend was our anniversary, too.

So when Toshiko-san gazed down at the tombstone instead of leaving and said how shocked "his sister Mitsuko-san" was when he died, all I could think was how many goddamn times had I had to hear her prattling about her?

"You mean his half sister," I said.

She peered at me through her bifocals. "What you say?"

"You said 'sister,'" I said, "when Mitsuko is my father's *half* sister. She's his stepmother's daughter. Eiko, my father's mother, had only one child—"

Toshiko-san interrupted. She was smiling, warm as ever, but insistent: she'd meant what she said. Feeling off balance and vaguely troubled, I let it drop.

I should have guessed the truth. Toshiko-san's English isn't perfect, but after half a century in America, she knows how to make herself understood. Yet when I called my mother the next day to ask if Eiko had a daughter as well as a son and she said yes—*I thought you knew*—I didn't believe it.

I asked how many years separated my father and Mitsuko.

"She was two years younger," my mother said, "maybe less."

"That can't be right," I said. "In the box of photos that I found, there were no pictures of a younger sister, and Daddy had to be four years plus in some of them—"

My mother didn't respond. Confused by my confusion, maybe, or just waiting until I caught on.

"Oh," I said. "Oh."

Eventually I'd admit that I, too, was to blame. I had a set image of my father as a child: privileged in a world populated by cooing adults, a sense that the photos had both reinforced and brought vividly to life. And why hadn't I known anything about my father's childhood? I hadn't cared. Maybe he and my mother *did* talk in my presence, or even to me directly, about his sister Mitsuko, and I didn't listen. After the call with my mother, I phoned my older sister, and when I asked if she'd known that Daddy had a younger sister, I could feel her eyeroll through the line. *Where have* you *been.*

Yet when my mother first confirmed the presence of a sister, I was furious—outraged that Mitsuko's parents and grandparents had taken so many photos of her brother and so few of her, and angry with my father. Couldn't he have gotten his hands on one pic of his little sis?

My anger surprised me. I shouldn't feel like that. God knows I'd heard enough about Japan's sexism.

I was reeling—my father had a sister!—and hours passed before it clicked. If there was an explanation for his unhappiness, his sister might hold the key.

I asked Toshiko-san for Mitsuko's contact info. She gave it to me with a warning. *Mitsuko-san—she like your father,* ne. *Depressed.* She would see it as her duty to meet with me, but I should expect little more.

That was fine with me. I was seeking answers, not the companionship of an aunt. I wrote Mitsuko-san an email, in English, introducing myself as Shoichi's second daughter and asking if I could call on her in Japan. *I found some old photos of my father and would be grateful for information about them.*

She responded within days. *Call me when you're in Tokyo and we can meet for lunch.* I booked a flight for early May, right after classes ended, and settled down to wait.

Tokyo was swampy, the sun a dull but potent glow, the day I met Mitsuko. The restaurant she selected was in Kashiwa, the suburb where she and her husband lived, on the top floor of a bustling *depato.*

The woman the hostess led me to was bone thin. In a restaurant and city teeming with well-dressed, carefully made-up women with dyed and coiffed 'dos, she had hair the same pure white as my father's: cut chin length, it was held in place with a black bobby pin. Her eyes were like pebbles, small and dark.

We exchanged bows, greetings, gifts, family chitchat—she said we'd met, but years ago, when I was too young to remember—and condolences. She remarked on my resemblance to my mother; neither of us, we agreed, looked like Shoichi. Then as I took notes, she answered my questions. Age: seventy-six. Now an English tutor, she had taught piano for decades. She had a husband who was a retired computer scientist and three children. She hadn't seen Shoichi for ten years, but they'd regularly phoned and emailed.

Her English was impeccable, far better than my father's, and she seemed both alert and intelligent. Yet I soon concluded that Toshiko-san was right. Mitsuko was depressed or sedated, perhaps both. Her voice was a low monotone, and she had a dull, almost leaden affect I recognized from my father during his long hospital stays.

Soon she was deep into a monologue about what a sweet, understanding brother Shoichi had been: "I adored him, he was the only consistently kind person of my childhood." When the waitress arrived, she barely stopped talking to order.

As I listened, I did my dutiful best, trying to picture my father through her eyes. A beloved older brother, an *onii-chan,* crouching protectively over her when she fell; taking her for a ride on the fancy toy car I'd seen in the photos; telling her to *go on, pet the doggie's head*, daijobu-yo, *he won't bite*. His face blocking out the sun as he smiled encouragingly at her; his wiry, little-boy arms shielding her and propping her up.

But the exercise left me cold. Everyone was innocent at one point; dig deep enough in any SOB's background and someone would turn up to say something nice.

When I interrupted to ask about how their mother's death had affected Shoichi, Mitsuko's expression didn't change.

"He barely knew her," she said. Their mother, Eiko, had been frail. Nursemaids took care of him from the day he was born. That Shoichi could remember her at all was unexpected. "I was only three when she died," Mitsuko said. "I can't recall a single thing."

I leaned forward, my pen and notepad forgotten. "Do you know what he remembered about her?"

"He said she had a gentle face."

"Nothing else?"

"No."

"Even so," I said, "she was his *mother*—"

Mitsuko was shaking her head. Of course mothers matter. Still, Eiko never breast-fed him. She'd held him only a few times. "So her death couldn't have that much impact on him."

"Are you sure?"

"Yes."

Her monotone and lack of affect were getting on my nerves.

"What about the war?" I asked. "The bomb scares, the near starvation Shoichi endured. That must have got to him—he must have found that traumatic."

"I don't think so." Mitsuko herself had been shipped out to the countryside to stay with her father's cousin, so she didn't know everything Shoichi had gone through. But everyone in Japan suffered. Shoichi was young. He'd bounced back. "When we met up at the end of the war, he seemed taller and thinner, but otherwise the same."

I drew wavy lines along the edge of my notebook, eyeing Mitsuko all the while. She seemed awfully sure of herself.

"I heard that my father's nursemaids spoiled him," I said. "I can't really blame them. He was so bright, and they must have pitied him, the poor motherless—"

Another headshake. "The nursemaids doted on him," she said. "He was loving and funny as well as smart, but hardly spoiled." Briefly her gaze slid away. "In fact, quite the opposite."

"Okay," I said, "how about—" But I was out of ideas. Shoichi had hurt and tormented us; he'd come home in a bad mood and, finding me on the phone, whacked me so hard across the face that my head hit the floor with a thud, my friend on the other end scared and confused (*Hello, hello? Are you there, what's going on?*); he'd held my mother's head to a lit stove until she was screaming, the air filling with the smell of singed hair and her face turning bright red, simply because he was sick. There was no other key to his character.

My father had been a man in the grip of brain chemistry, no more, no less.

I looked down at the few words I'd scrawled on my notepad. I wanted nothing more than to return to my tiny hotel room, crawl under the covers, and phone Rob and bawl.

"Are you okay?"

I glanced up. Mitsuko's eyes were wide.

"I'm fine," I said.

"Really?" she said. "It seems like—" She pursed her lips. "Can I get you anything?"

"No, that's—" I began. "Actually, some dessert would be great. Thank you."

Her smile was shy.

As she beckoned the waitress, I sat back. What was I doing? Mitsuko was old and I didn't travel often to Japan. How many more conversations would I have with her?

I'd been so hell-bent on cracking the riddle of my father that I'd almost missed the chance to hear the story of his childhood. I forgot to ask about the storyteller herself.

We arrived at the topic of my mother through a circuitous route. Mitsuko said that in the sixties her husband had landed a professorship in computer science in a small college in the American South, but because he wasn't able to get tenure, they'd eventually moved back to Japan.

"He must be very smart," I said. "A professorship—"

"He was never more than average," Mitsuko said. "Certainly nothing like Shoichi." She drained her tea. "He and I have little in common. It hasn't been a happy marriage."

I was taken aback—she was so frank—but did my best not to show it. "I'm sorry to hear that. At least you have your children."

"Two live in America. One lives close by, but I hardly ever see him."

"That's hard. Maybe you could come to America and visit—"

"My husband has Alzheimer's. Really he should be in a nursing home. But he's my husband, so I stay in Tokyo and take care of him."

"I'm so sorry—" I trailed off. She was watching me, her pebble eyes unreadable. She wasn't asking for my pity, that was clear. Her words had washed me back to my mother, and the very different choice that she'd made with her sick husband. Was that Mitsuko's point? Was she drawing a line between herself and my mother?

The thought was ridiculous. Why would she do that? I was being ungenerous. Mitsuko was here to help me understand my past. She was on my side.

As if her thoughts had kept pace with mine, she said, "Your mother remarried, didn't she? Is she well?"

"She lives in England," I said, following up with the usual about my stepfather, her books, and her health. I said again, as I had at the start of our meeting, that she sent her regards.

"We were never close, your mother and I," Mitsuko said.

"Well, with her in America and you in Japan—"

"My husband and I were living in North Carolina when Shoichi and your mother were in Princeton," Mitsuko said. "It was before you were born. We saw each other a lot then."

"I didn't realize. My mother never told me."

"Your mother—" There was a sly look in her eye. "Do you know the term *ojosan*? It means something like little princess," she said. "Your mother came from a better family and class than Shoichi and I did. She couldn't understand us. She couldn't comprehend what we'd been through."

I didn't know what to say. There was no way my mother's family's wealth could have compared with Mitsuko's and my father's. My mother and her five siblings had grown up in a roomy but hardly fancy home, and their parents had one or two servants while my father's parents had dozens. Had Mitsuko been led astray by my mother's elegance and bearing, or was there something else going on? Was that look in her eyes slyness or malice?

I was about to inform her that she was mistaken when it came to me.

Mitsuko hadn't been acting out of malice. She was trying to assert and, perhaps, avenge herself.

Growing up, she'd had little. Motherless and the middle child, perpetually overshadowed by brilliant, charismatic Shoichi and her stepmother's children. And a girl. Being cut from the will and cheated of his share of the inheritance had enraged my father. Mitsuko had never been in the will at all.

But even though her *onii-san* had more than her, she'd seen him as her ally. And in this, she wasn't wrong. They were underdogs, banded together in a hardscrabble world. When my mother left and divorced my father, naturally Mitsuko had taken his side, casting my mother as the villain.

Or maybe that was just the final strike against my mother. Why hadn't I known that my father had a sister? Their family's bias against daughters had meant there were no photos of Mitsuko in my father's stash. I was to blame for my indifference to my father's childhood. Another factor was my mother. She, who'd told me hundreds of stories about my father, had no tales of his sister.

My mother had looked down on Mitsuko. Sitting across the table from my aunt, I knew that for a fact. In part this was because my mother—who'd wanted a son so badly she wept and plunged into a month-long depression after giving birth to her third daughter—couldn't help but absorb some of her culture's prejudice against women. In part because she, stylish as well as accomplished, would have thought Mitsuko too quiet and unambitious, too lacking in brilliance, vivacity, and verve—a woman who wore bobby pins, and in the wrong color!

And Mitsuko, smart, thin-skinned, and proud, had felt my mother's disdain and burned.

By the time I spread the photos on the table, I'd already heard how Mitsuko's grandmother, out of concern for her son's second wife, methodically rooted through the family albums, throwing out every image of Eiko. But even if I couldn't see my father's mother's face, I was eager to see Mitsuko react to the pictures. Looking them over, she betrayed little emotion, but perhaps they weren't without impact: as she talked, she grew more animated, the color rising in her cheeks.

"The big house in this picture," she said, tapping on the table next to it. "Shoichi and I grew up here. It belonged to my grandparents, but we lived Japanese-style, several generations all together."

The photo showed Shoichi and an Akita puppy framed by the grand house.

"It was a special place," Mitsuko said. Light and airy, and filled with Japanese and Chinese art and precious objects. In the central room were old scrolls that had been in the family for generations. "My grandmother said they were priceless."

I asked where the house was.

"Kojimachi—do you know it?"

I nodded, suppressing the urge to whistle. Kojimachi, one of the most fashionable, high-rent districts of Tokyo: on a cab ride through the neighborhood, I'd craned my head upward to take in the glittering stores, high-rises, embassies, and hotels.

"The house was famous for its fine proportions and gardens," Mitsuko said. "It was three stories high, and covered a lot of ground."

Encircling her teacup with both hands, she said, "Like so much else in Tokyo, it didn't make it through the war."

Because Kojimachi was near the Imperial Palace, she said, it was one of the safer neighborhoods, with antiaircraft guns aimed at the sky at all times. But one night in May 1945, a plane that had been shot down crashed onto their house. Although everyone somehow got out in time—Mitsuko had been in the countryside, but her father, stepmother, and Shoichi had been there, as well as one remaining servant—the house and everything inside it burned to the ground.

"The problem," Mitsuko said, "was that in those days, everything was made of wood. In the war, with all that bombing—Tokyo never had a chance."

I looked up from my note taking. Time and again, I'd heard my mother express the same sentiment. Yet her tone was always wistful—*You can't even imagine how different Tokyo was back then*—her gaze faraway. Mitsuko sounded matter-of-fact, and her eyes were fixed on me.

"But that was the war," she said, straightening her back. "In the years before that, our family lived a different kind of life."

Her father, Hisa, had been a professor in the medical department at the University of Tokyo. Her grandfather—Mitsuko pointed to a couple of the shots of the egg-headed man—was a famous stomach surgeon who'd studied in Germany. He owned and ran a very big hospital. Mitsuko's grandmother, the woman I'd mistaken for Eiko, was smart and kind and did secretarial work at her husband's hospital. At home dozens of maids and servants worked around the clock to satisfy the family's every need.

"To an outsider looking in," Mitsuko said, "our life probably seemed ideal."

She was six when her father announced he was getting remarried. She was already a devoted piano student, so when she learned that her stepmother-to-be was a Julliard-trained concert pianist, she couldn't believe her luck.

Her name was Haruko. She moved in with six trunks of clothes, four boxes of sheet music, and a Steinway grand, one of the few in Japan at the time, so big it barely fit into a six tatami-mat room. Haruko loved classical composers, Chopin her particular favorite, but the war had started by then, and national fervor forbade all but Japanese and German music. The neighbors complained about her, even though she stayed away from Chopin, maybe because they knew she hadn't gotten rid of her sheet music, maybe just because she had a Steinway.

"They probably weren't all that sorry," Mitsuko said, "that the piano burned along with the house."

Around us the restaurant din rose and receded. "Why did you say your life only seemed ideal?" I asked. "Were you referring to your mother's illness, or the war?"

"Neither," Mitsuko said. "The truth was that it wasn't easy being raised by nursemaids. With so many coming and going"—she gestured at one of the photos of the girls in aprons—"Shoichi and I had no sense of stability. Our grandparents were loving but old, and busy with the hospital." She hunched her narrow shoulders. "It was a lonely life."

"But what about your father?" I said. "I thought Hisa raised the two of—"

"He didn't." Her face was impassive.

"When your mother died, wasn't he—"

"He left almost immediately after she died." His destination was Rochester, New York. Hisa did research there for more than a year and probably would have stayed longer, Mitsuko said, had it not been for the war. As it was, he'd been on the last ship transporting Japanese back to Japan.

"But—" I hesitated, feeling confused. "Why would he leave the two of you then?" I asked. "Was he unable to bear being home with Eiko gone?"

"I guess that's possible," Mitsuko said, her tone implying the opposite.

Like his father, Hisa had trained as a doctor, she said. Yet he had little interest in practicing medicine, never mind that his father's dearest wish was that his son take over his hospital. In Rochester Hisa had studied isotopes and radiation therapy. Later, in 1945, he was one of the first scientists sent to Hiroshima after the bomb was dropped. He stayed three days, and the radioactivity he was exposed to weakened his bones and veins. When he died, suddenly, at seventy-one, the doctors said it was a factor.

"Is there a picture of him?" I asked.

"Just one." The photo she picked up showed a young man sitting on the steps of the house. Dressed in a *yukata*, or light summer kimono, he had small squinty eyes, wire-framed glasses, and hair shorn close to his head. Crooked teeth crowded his mouth. Life was good: sunlight slanted down and the garden was glorious; I could almost hear the high-pitched whine of the cicadas. A few feet away, Shoichi, a cherubic toddler, knitted his brow in concentration as he hoisted a toy truck almost half his size. Yet the man looked ill at ease, his grin strained, his body tense.

Mitsuko said, "He was ugly, wasn't he."

I had to smile. "He was."

"What you can't tell from the photo is that he was ugly inside as well as out." Although her voice was still low, it wasn't quite as even, and I turned toward her.

"He was an unstable man," she said. "Our grandparents were kind people, but when it came to their son, too indulgent." They'd had trouble bearing children—they had two sons early on, but both had died, one in childbirth and the other when he was a few months old—and they'd just about given up hope.

"And then Hisa was born," Mitsuko said. "So maybe it wasn't all that surprising that he grew up to be an awful father."

My mouth felt dry. "Are you saying—did he mistreat you and Shoichi in some way?"

Her nod was short. "He beat us. Often, and often for the smallest reason." The beatings, which had begun soon after his return from America, became worse after he remarried, Mitsuko said. The stepmother, who disliked her and Shoichi, egged him on.

"Shoichi, as the eldest, had it the worst," Mitsuko said. "Sometimes our father would take him to a room, hit him over and over, and then lock him up and leave him alone for hours."

A part of me wanted to say that couldn't have happened. Look at how many pictures there are of Shoichi, don't you see all his beautiful outfits and toys, how the adults throng around him? But I didn't need my aunt to tell me that I was conflating the Japanese worship of sons with love.

Later, going over this conversation with my mother, I'd ask if my father ever hinted that Hisa was cruel. She'd begin shaking her head and then all at once her face would change. *There was this one time.* She'd tell me how, when we were living in Tokyo and Shoichi had his breakdown during the big fusion conference in Italy, Hisa and his stepmother had met them at Haneda Airport afterward and taken them to a hotel to regroup. While there, Shoichi had screamed at his father about how terrible he'd been to him throughout his childhood. *I've gone mad because of you.* But he was raving by then—my mother was imprisoning him; Martians were marshaling armies against him—and so, my mother would say, she paid his words no heed.

"My father hit me a lot, too," Mitsuko said.

Her hands were clasped on the table.

"Dinners were particularly stressful," she said. "I was so scared, I used to wet myself during them."

Her face had been so expressionless, it was a shock to see it crumple.

"That's terrible," I said.

She nodded, blinking away her tears.

"You shouldn't have had to go through that," I said. "No one should. My father—" I broke off.

I wanted to tell her that he hit us. More than a year ago, I'd told Toshiko-san and it had forged a bond between us, something good that came out of what we'd endured.

But I couldn't say that to Mitsuko. When she first talked about what a kind brother Shoichi had been, I'd assumed she was trying to reassure me, but she was just telling the truth. She had adored him. She still did. He was the one constant in a life filled with chaos, and probably he had been kind to her. Why tarnish her one pure memory? She didn't need to know that he ended up resembling their father.

"What were you going to say about Shoichi?" Mitsuko asked. She'd already recovered—her eyes dry, composure back—and once again I was conscious that she was watching me closely.

"Nothing," I said. "I'm just sorry he had to go through that, too."

She kept her pebble eyes on me a moment more. Then she glanced away, her sigh almost inaudible. "Yes, those were difficult years for him."

With the lunch crowd gone, the restaurant was just about empty. There was a window open at the far end of the room, and I realized that it was raining, a violent, monsoon-like deluge, and its steady beat or the damp warmth or smell of the air brought me back to a forgotten moment from the years I'd spent in Tokyo as a child: sitting on the floor and laughing with my father as the rain pelted down outside a half-open sliding door, the smooth springiness of tatami under my palms and thighs.

Mitsuko set down her teacup. "You know how Shoichi was always so nice to everyone—from the prime minister to the lowliest of servants?"

I nodded.

"I always thought that was a result of his childhood. His eagerness to please—it was the mark of someone who wasn't happy or comfortable with himself."

"I can see that."

"If you're beaten," she said, "and you're sure your parent loves you, you'll be okay. And if one parent beats you, but you know that the other one loves you, you'll also be all right."

I felt confused. Unlike Mitsuko, my father remembered their mother; he'd known he had a parent who loved him. Mitsuko's words didn't make sense—unless she wasn't talking about my father, but me.

"But if you have only one parent," Mitsuko continued, "and that parent beats you and doesn't love you, that's something else. That's a poison that's hard to recover from."

Poison. I thought of how abuse spreads, taking over a person. The message, *you're worth nothing,* planted through beatings as well as words, creeping inside, taking root, and growing until nothing else can.

I thought of the small boy with the Dumbo ears, and then the older version—the searching eyes, the anxious grin.

Something inside me was cracking open. My heart, I thought.

Mitsuko's lips twitched upward. "Shoichi could be difficult. I can imagine you had trouble with him. But he was so proud of you. Your books, your PhD."

"My father—" My breath caught. "He was sick."

She brushed that aside. "You had good times. I know you did." Her voice held what might have been a pleading note. "You remember them, don't you?"

My eyes were brimming over. Yet my mind felt clearer than it had for a long time.

"I'm trying," I said.

Later, back in my tiny hotel room, I phoned Rob. I wanted to convey something I'd dimly grasped during my conversation with Mitsuko, something I should have known all along: there was no key to my father. He was elusive and capacious, as all of us are, every memory I had of him refracting, shifting over time and with the light.

So I told Rob a story.

I was in my early twenties, and my father and I were on a bench at the Jersey shore. We were alone, Ellie and my younger sister having gone ahead to the diner for breakfast. The wind was gusting; the gray of the ocean blurred with the sky so that the lone cruise ship we could see seemed suspended on the horizon, aloft.

He and I had been having a better or at least less terrible time than usual, with even a shared laugh or two about the other's enslavement to coffee, and on impulse I asked a question I'd been pondering for some time.

"Did you wake me up to watch the moon landing? That's what I remember," I said, "but sometimes I think I imagined it."

I thought he'd say I was dreaming or what was somehow worse, that he didn't recall. But he nodded his giant head, his gaze fixed on the ship.

"It was a big night," he said. "Everyone was watching."

"Including me?"

"I don't know. You were on your mother's lap."

I felt disappointed, by myself as much as by him. This was my father, for Chrissakes. What was I expecting? Would I never learn?

Still, I couldn't quite give up. "Did you say anything to me?"

"Like what?"

The wind, tangy with salt, was whipping my hair in my face. My father was only in his fifties, but he looked far older, and tired and weak. He had bags under his eyes; his wrists and ankles were like sticks. I wanted to think he was bewildered or even just puzzled, but his expression was blank. Incurious.

"Forget it," I said, leaving him behind to join the others.

But that was then.

The moon landing was my earliest memory—I was three—and I hadn't made it up. My father, a man who was to the end intoxicated by stars and the possibilities of space travel, had been in his mid-thirties: lit with the potential of science and, at the height of his powers, confident that groundbreaking discoveries and successes lay within his reach. The night was the most eagerly anticipated and exhilarating of his life, and he'd thought to include me. Yes, he offloaded the dozing toddler that I was onto my mother. But she, always practical, worn out by the demands of two small children and aware that I'd remember little, if at all, would have argued for letting me sleep, and he overrode her protests.

He might not have said the words I thought I remembered, but as he lifted me, drowsy and warm, and carried me to the living room, maybe a version of them ran through his mind. *Tonight will change the world forever. You'll never forget what you see for the rest of your life.* And even if he ended up handing me off to my mother, I didn't dream the sensation that something momentous was happening beyond the screen doors, somewhere high in the sky. I didn't invent drifting off in his arms as he stood gazing upward, hushed and rapt.

ACKNOWLEDGMENTS

My heartfelt gratitude to all those who told me stories, checked the science, read drafts, gave suggestions, and provided support and friendship over the long years I've spent on this book: Toshiko Abram, Lan Samantha Chang, Susan Cheever, T. K. Chu, Frank Cipriani, Jean Kephart Cipriani, Sam Cohen, Susan Fisher, Julie Glass, David Groff, Richard Hoffman, Paul Horowitz, Alex Johnson, Daphne Kalotay, Sandra Lim, Margot Livesey, Megan Marshall, Kyoko Mori, Elisse Ota, Rick Reiken, Julie Rold, Andrea Rutherford, Marian Sabal, Matilda Sabal, Max Sabal, Jane Shattuc, Ali Sherwin, Miranda Sherwin, Hazel Stix, Mitsuko Suzuki, Larry Tribe, Jerald Walker, Shujen Wang, Elizabeth Westling, Joan Wickersham, Stephanie Wrobel, Steve Yarbrough, and Eve Zimmerman.

This book would not be possible without Kristen Elias Rowley, the most brilliant, capable, and warm editor I've ever had the pleasure of working with: why she isn't running the world already stupefies me. Kathy Daneman and Samara Rafert are extraordinary publicists, resourceful and enterprising.

Parts of this book have appeared, often in modified form, as essays in journals and anthologies:

Harvard Review: "Tokyo Monsoon"
LitHub: "A Monster No Matter What"

Missouri Review and *Best American Essays*: "My Father's Women"

Missouri Review: "Chess Superhero" and "The Veterans Project Number Two"

Southern Indiana Review and *Every Father's Daughter*: "Secrets of the Sun"

Southern Indiana Review: "Clothes Make the Man"

Story and *Longreads*: "Jersey Girl"

I'm beholden to the editors who made that possible: Evelyn Rogers Somers and Speer Morgan of the *Missouri Review*, Ron Mitchell of *Southern Indiana Review*, Christina Thompson of *Harvard Review*, Michael Nye of *Story*, Tim Denevi of *LitHub*, Robert Atwan of *Best American Essays*, Aaron Gilbreath of *Longreads*, and Margaret McMullan of the anthology *Every Father's Daughter*.

The Virginia Center for the Creative Arts, which awarded me the Goldfarb Family Fellowship; Emerson College; and Judy and Bob Huret, whose generous fellowship I was lucky enough to receive twice, gave me the best gift of all for a writer, time.

My brave, loving mother, Hiroko Sherwin, a source of awe and wonder, revisited the most painful moments of her past again and again to help me understand my father. My stepfather, James Sherwin, has rescued me more times and in more ways than I can count, and I will be ever grateful for his wisdom and guidance.

To Rob Sabal, my husband, who listened, held me, and never wavered through a turbulent first year: what great good fortune to go through life with you. What joy.

Finally, to my father, Shoichi Yoshikawa: *Gomen nasai.* May you rest in peace.

21st Century Essays
David Lazar and Patrick Madden, Series Editors

This series from Mad Creek Books is a vehicle to discover, publish, and promote some of the most daring, ingenious, and artistic nonfiction. This is the first and only major series that announces its focus on the essay—a genre whose plasticity, timelessness, popularity, and centrality to nonfiction writing make it especially important in the field of nonfiction literature. In addition to publishing the most interesting and innovative books of essays by American writers, the series publishes extraordinary international essayists and reprint works by neglected or forgotten essayists, voices that deserve to be heard, revived, and reprised. The series is a major addition to the possibilities of contemporary literary nonfiction, focusing on that central, frequently chimerical, and invariably supple form: The Essay.

*Annual Gournay Prize Winner